Paper Birds

25+ Projects to Copy, Cut, and Fold

Hiroshi Hayakawa

LARK

LARK

An Imprint of Sterling Publishing
387 Park Avenue South
New York, NY 10016

ISBN 978-1-4547-0845-2

Library of Congress Cataloging-in-Publication Data

Hayakawa, Hiroshi, 1962-
  Paper birds : 25+ projects to copy, cut, and fold / Hiroshi Hayakawa.
    pages cm
  Summary: "Origami takes flight with these 30 beautiful bird projects, from a cockatiel, horned
owl, and hummingbird to the exotic albatross and extinct dodo. Just photocopy the templates
onto cardstock; score, cut, and fold; and, finally, interlock the joints to create a dimensional crea-
ture. All the projects are arranged by difficulty and the richly photographed pages show the birds
from multiple perspectives, perching, standing, and flying. "-- Provided by publisher.
  ISBN 978-1-4547-0845-2 (pbk.)
 1. Origami. 2. Paper bird making. I. Title.
  TT872.5.H39 2014
  736'.982--dc23
                              2013035872

Distributed in Canada by Sterling Publishing
c/o Canadian Manda Group, 165 Dufferin Street
Toronto, Ontario, Canada M6K 3H6
Distributed in the United Kingdom by GMC Distribution Services
Castle Place, 166 High Street, Lewes, East Sussex, England BN7 1XU
Distributed in Australia by Capricorn Link (Australia) Pty. Ltd.
P.O. Box 704, Windsor, NSW 2756, Australia

For information about custom editions, special sales, and premium and corporate purchases,
please contact Sterling Special Sales at 800-805-5489 or specialsales@sterlingpublishing.com.

Email academic@larkbooks.com for information about desk and examination copies.
The complete policy can be found at larkcrafts.com.

Manufactured in China

2 4 6 8 10 9 7 5 3 1

larkcrafts.com

Contents

Introduction

The world of birds is full of wonders. The colorful, feathery dresses birds such as peacocks or hummingbirds wear could put today's top fashion designers to shame. Some of the migratory birds' uncanny ability to perfectly navigate the Earth and fly thousands of miles from one destination to another year after year beats any high-tech GPS systems we have. The way the owl's night vision allows it to catch its prey at night is nothing short of astonishing. However, what is remarkable about the world of birds is not just their abilities beyond our imagination, but also their unique relationships with us humans. Parrots are known for understanding our language and emotions. We all know about the pigeons' service to humankind when they delivered messages during war times. In many cultures, certain birds are viewed and worshipped as symbols of hope, freedom, or messengers from heaven. In the art of falconry, the bird is not just subservient; man and bird hunt together. Birds are a reminder of our connection to nature. They show us what they are capable of, make us reflect on what they mean to us, and in doing so rekindle our deep longing to be one with nature.

All the projects in this book were designed using two types of traditional paper craft techniques: *Origami* and *kirigami*. Origami means "paper folding" and kirigami means "paper cutting" in Japanese. In this book, I will show you how to combine these two techniques to create birds that are three-dimensional and full of details. These techniques involve three very distinct processes: scoring, cutting, and folding. For this book I added a fourth process to a few projects, which is gluing. Because of the unique physical characteristics of some of the birds, I decided it would be beneficial to include this extra step to make the construction of them a little friendlier for my readers. Although they all have interlocking joints that give them enough structural strength to stand alone without adhesive, a little bit of glue will add extra strength and, in some cases, help add details that are essential to identify those particular species.

Before you pick up a pair of scissors and start cutting, read the next chapter, How to Use This Book. The process for making each bird is the same: Photocopy or print the project template (or templates), and follow the step-by-step instructions and illustrations to score, cut, fold, and shape the paper into a dimensional (and expressive) bird. Some of the projects might look a bit intimidating at first, but you'll discover that the process of carefully shaping paper is actually quite simple and even meditative! So familiarize yourself with the basic steps, and then begin creating!

The projects in this book are grouped by skill level: very easy, easy, intermediate, and advanced. If you are new to kirigami, I suggest you start with the easiest bird projects before you work your way to the more complex ones.

I hope first and foremost that you will have fun making the birds in this book. I also hope this book will play a little role in reminding you of our often-forgotten connection to nature and help you start imagining what we can do to get connected again.

Hiroshi Hayakawa

How to Use This Book

You might think that creating 25+ projects out of paper would require quite the collection of techniques and tools, but the reality is rather simple: Each of these birds is made by scoring, cutting, folding, and shaping paper, and you'll need only a few basic tools to get going! This section of the book thoroughly explores basic kirigami techniques as well as some tips to help you along the way. The projects' step-by-step illustrations and templates include symbols that explain where to cut, fold, and so on, and you'll find a descriptive explanation of those symbols in the following pages. While the construction of each bird is based on its physical shape and traits, you're the artist when it comes to adding color and detail to your paper bird. Feel free to reference the project photos for color inspiration, or personalize your bird with the markings and patterns of your preference.

Although the design of each bird is different, the first two steps in making each bird—scoring and cutting—are exactly the same for all of them. I have described these steps here rather than repeating them in every set of project instructions, so please read this section thoroughly before you begin.

WORKING WITH THE TEMPLATES

Every project in this book begins with a full-size template, found on pages 95-126. Keep in mind that the template details are meant to be printed on the reverse side (or underside) of your paper; make sure you score and cut on the printed side. Once you've constructed the birds, most of the printed folding lines won't be visible on their outer surfaces.

Photocopy the templates instead of using the originals. This way, you will be able to make as many birds as you like. How about filling a birdcage with your favorite birds? Wouldn't it be wonderful if you made a diorama with Macaws in all possible shade and color combinations? The possibilities are endless.

PAPER

The type of paper you should use needs to be thin enough to be easily folded yet sturdy enough to give structural strength to the birds. With this in mind, you'll need to copy the project templates onto cardstock rather than regular printer paper. All of the projects in *Paper Birds* were made with cardstock, which you can easily find at your local office supply or craft store. The Hummingbird and Peacock were made with metallic vellum. The paper's reflective surface is appropriate for the look of iridescent feathers that those two birds have. The use of vellum is optional—you can of course create them using regular cardstock paper.

There are a variety of cardstock thicknesses, colors, shades, and textures to choose from. Stay away from inexpensive cardstock that may have a white core in the center: When you score and fold such paper, the white core will appear in your fold. To photocopy or print on cardstock, adjust the printer's paper setting, and, depending on your printer, you might want to hand feed the cardstock one sheet at a time to avoid jamming.

SYMBOLS

As you work on the projects, you'll need to understand the symbols that appear on the templates and in the illustrations that come with the assembly instructions. These are shown and described below.

A transition from one step to the next

Move a part of the template or a tool in the direction of the arrow

Movement occurs toward/on the reverse side of the template

Turn over a part of the template, reversing the inside/outside relationship

Create a rounded surface with a dowel

Create a curved surface with a dowel. The shape of the arrow indicates the general shape and the direction of the curve.

Enlarged view of a smaller section

Indicates ups and downs of the surface levels after a series of folds

Turn over the entire template

SCORING

Scoring is the act of creating lines and edges in paper that will facilitate folding and shaping: Scoring is the first step in making any of the birds (yes, even before cutting out a template). You'll score the folding lines first, which are indicated by dashed and dotted lines on a template.

Scoring makes folding easier and neater later on. If you cut out the template first, scoring these lines, especially in a small, delicate area, is sometimes more difficult, so it's best to score first.

Begin by placing the template on a smooth, flat, hard surface. A surface that's too soft, such as newspaper, may cause you to dig deep grooves into the template as you score, which would make the assembled bird unsightly.

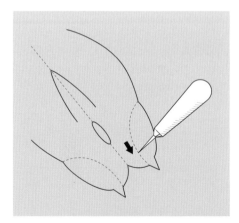

Figure 1

The key to successful scoring is to avoid exerting too much pressure on your scoring tool. Score the folding lines with an awl, a small nail, a bone folder, a ballpoint pen that's run out of ink, or anything else with a hard, pointed tip (figure 1). Even though some of the scored lines will be folded downward and others will be folded upward, score them all on the same printed side of the template. Try not to stray from the marked lines. You want to be especially careful when you score the lines around the ankles of the freestanding birds. Many of those birds have skinny legs, and if you score the ankle folding lines too hard, they might lose the strength they need in their legs to stand securely on the ground.

To make scoring straight lines easier, use the edge of a ruler as a guide (figure 2).

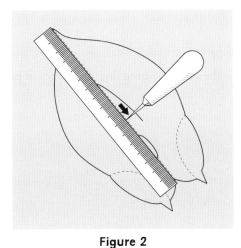

Figure 2

CUTTING

After you've scored the folding lines, you'll begin cutting. The solid lines on the templates represent the cutting lines.

First, use a craft knife to cut along all the solid lines within the interior perimeter of the template. These lines include small cuts along the eyes, the beak of some of the birds, and the cutting lines of the tabs for interlocking joints. When making small, curved cuts such as those for the beak of the Barn Owl (Barn Owl project is available online. See page 128 for details.), rotate the paper in the opposite direction as the movement of your knife (figure 3).

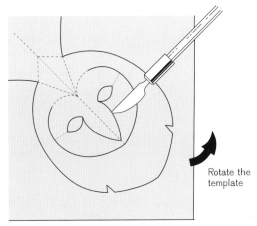

Rotate the template

Figure 3

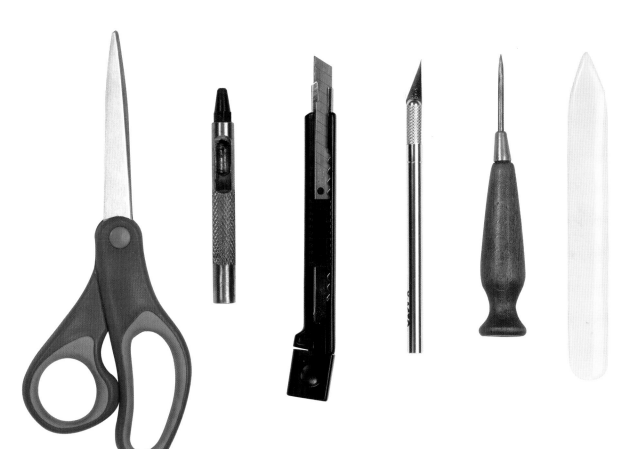

Be very careful when using a craft knife; keep your hand away from the path of the blade. A small child may need an adult's help when making precision cuts.

Next, use a pair of scissors or a craft knife to cut along the contour perimeter of the template (figure 4).

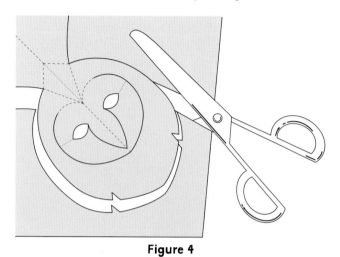

Figure 4

When cutting away small, sharp areas that extend beyond the template's contour but toward the interior (the Dodo's feet shown below is a good example), first use scissors to make a rough cut (figure 5), remove the template from the page, and then cut away the remaining paper with a craft knife, moving the instrument from the interior toward the exterior (figure 6).

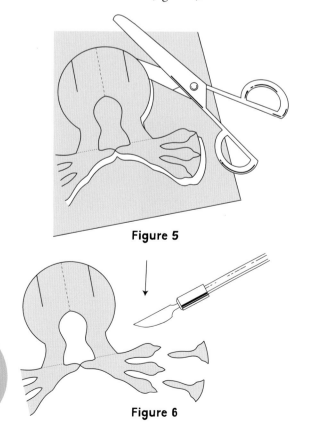

Figure 5

Figure 6

Cutting a straight line is easy. Use the edge of a ruler as a guide—the same as when you are scoring a straight line—and cut along the line with a craft knife. Use a metal ruler so that you don't damage its edge with the blade (figure 7).

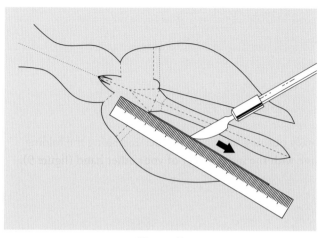

Figure 7

To cut out small circles such as the eyes of the Dove (page 54), you can use a craft knife, but the best tool for this job is a paper (or leather) punch (figure 8).

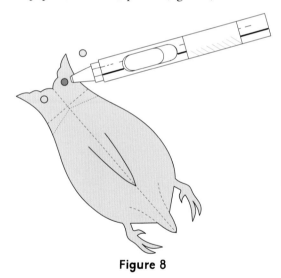

Figure 8

Select a tip of the right size, align the tip of the punch with the circle you are cutting out, and gently tap the end of the tool with a wooden or rubber mallet.

FOLDING

Now that you've scored and cut out the project template, you'll begin the really fun part: folding. This is when the bird actually begins to take shape into a dimensional object. Two types of folds are used in this book—the *peak fold* and the *valley fold*. A peak fold is represented by a dotted line, a valley fold by a line of dashes. Most folding can be done with your fingers, but small, delicate sections will require a little help from some tools.

Making a Peak Fold

Use the index finger and the thumb of one hand to push down on both sides of the dotted line, while simultaneously pushing up the area under and along the folding line with the index finger of your other hand (figure 9).

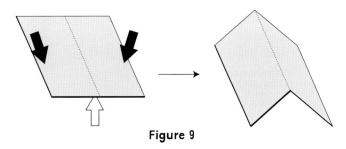

Figure 9

If the section of the template that calls for this type of fold is too small to use the edge of your finger, use a small tool, such as a toothpick, a needle, or the awl that you used for scoring.

Making a Valley Fold

Use one finger to push down along the dashed line of the template, while pushing up both sides of the folding line with the index finger and the thumb of your other hand (figure 10). Again, if the section to be folded is too small for your finger, push down the folding line with a small scoring tool instead.

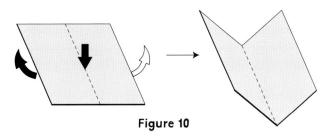

Figure 10

Folding a Curved Line

To fold a line that isn't straight, use your thumb and index finger to pinch and squeeze along opposing sides of the folding line while pushing the area under and along the folding line with the index finger of your other hand (figure 11).

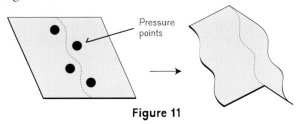

Pressure points

Figure 11

Making a Pocket Fold

Pocket folding—a combination of a peak fold and a valley fold—is typically used to form the neck-shoulder and tail-hip connections of many birds in this book. The figure below illustrates how to make this fold (figure 12).

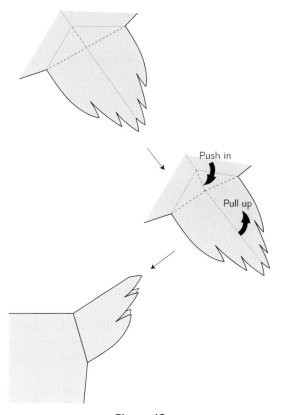

Push in

Pull up

Figure 12

SHAPING

These projects are designed to capture each bird's unique pose and expression, and some require the use of a few simple shaping techniques. These techniques aren't applicable to all the birds in this book, but using them adds an extra sense of realism and character to your work.

The first technique is used to round the body of a bird. After cutting out the template, turn it over. Use one hand to press the template against the edge of a desk or a table, and use the other hand to pull it back and forth across the edge a couple of times. This will add a natural curve to the bird's body (figure 13).

To create a nice, smooth curve in a small area of a template, roll it over a dowel (figure 14). A dowel produces a much neater result than rolling the template with your fingers. If you don't have a dowel, substitute a round pencil or any other thin, tubular object.

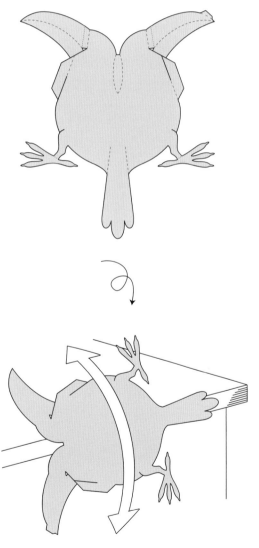

Figure 13

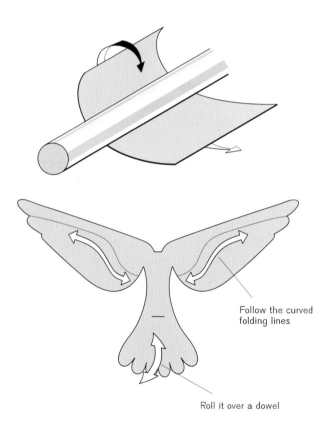

Follow the curved folding lines

Roll it over a dowel

Figure 14

10

JOINTS AND GLUE

Many of the birds in this book are held together by means of interlocking joints. They make it possible to assemble the birds without using glue or tape and provide the birds with enough strength (figure 15).

However, a few birds in this book require a small amount of glue to hold the shapes together. If glue is needed, it is indicated in the illustrations by gray shading, and you will learn exactly where you need to apply it (figure 16). Use common white glue or craft glue when it is called for, and when applying the glue to a small surface, use the tip of a cotton swab or toothpick for precision. This is optional, but you can also use a little bit of glue when you cross the tabs at the bases of the wings for some of the flying birds (figure 17).

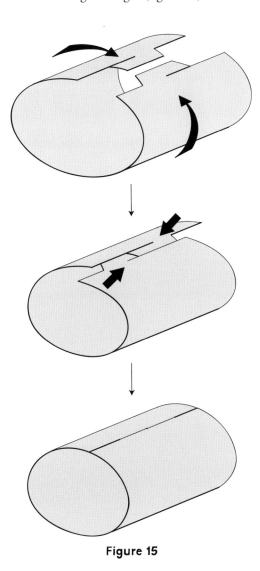

Figure 15

Glue on the other side

Figure 16

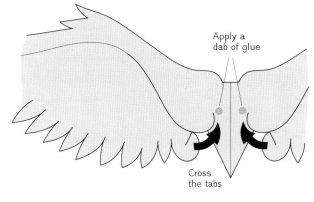

Apply a dab of glue

Cross the tabs

Figure 17

COLORING

The markings of many birds are very distinctive. I have included variations of birds in the project shots in this book. You can study the samples in the photographs and design your own versions when applying colors to the birds. Of course, you can be more intuitive about color choices and use any colors or unusual markings on them if you'd like. How about making Doves in multiple colors and turning them into a mobile?

You can use any opaque paint or drawing medium, as long as it isn't oil based. Acrylic paint, poster paint, tempera, watercolor, colored pencils, and pastels will all work just fine.

DISPLAY METHODS

There are three different groups of birds, based on the way they're displayed. The first group is the birds that are freestanding. You don't need anything special to display them. When one of these projects is completed, the last step is to adjust the angles of the legs so that the bird will stand comfortably on its feet without falling over. Some birds in this group have long tails and, although they are freestanding, they might need a low stand underneath their feet (figure 18). You can improvise and come up with your own material for the base: a block of wood, a rock, a stack of paper, etc. Learn if the bird you are going to make requires this type of base or not by studying the project photos.

The second group is the birds that are depicted in flight. You will need a thread (or thin wire) to hang these by. An X on the template indicates where to run the thread (figure 19).

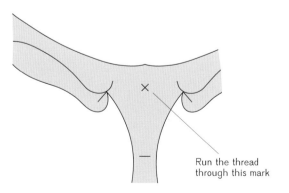

Figure 18

Run the thread through this mark

Figure 19

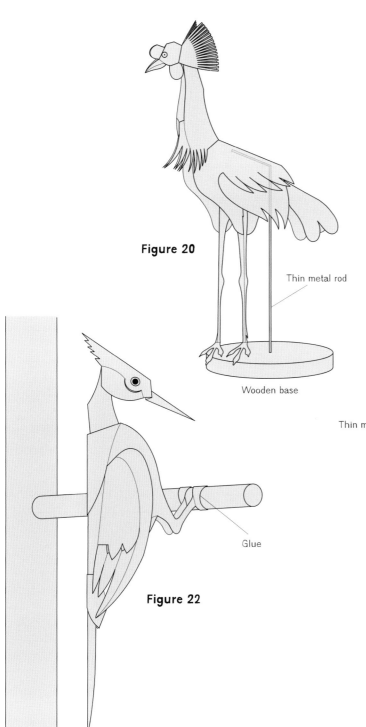

Figure 20

Thin metal rod

Wooden base

The third group is the birds that are not in flight, but require a customized display stand. There are four birds in this group: Flamingo, Roadrunner, Woodpecker, and Crowned Crane (the Crowned Crane can be found online, see page 128 for details). Some designs for simple display stands are illustrated below. Drill a tiny hole into a wooden base you can find at a craft store or hardware store, and insert a thin (32-or 16-gauge) metal rod bent at the right place for the height of the bird so that its feet will touch the ground when displayed (figures 20 and 21). For displaying the Woodpecker, you will need a vertical stand. This may be a piece of natural wood, a dowel, etc. You can either glue the bird's feet to the surface of the stand or use a tree branch for the bird to wrap its feet around (figure 22).

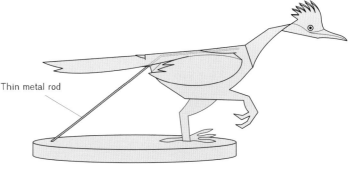

Thin metal rod

Figure 21

Glue

Figure 22

SELECTING A PROJECT

The projects in *Paper Birds* range in skill level from Very Easy to Advanced, and while they all employ the same basic techniques, it's always a good idea to practice a bit before diving right into a challenging or intricate design. If you're new to paper-cutting and folding crafts, or if you are a youngster, I recommend getting your feet wet by starting with the simpler birds in the Very Easy group and gradually moving on to more detailed birds as you practice and develop your skills.

Canada Goose

Once almost extinct, the Canada Goose has made a big comeback. Some of the naturally migrating geese overwinter on golf courses, in parks, and even in shopping malls.

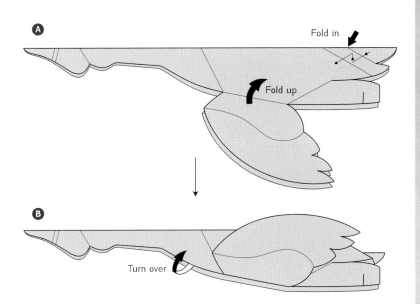

1 Using the Goose template on page 95, score the folding lines, then cut along all the solid lines, including the tabs for an interlocking joint, as depicted in How to Use This Book on pages 5-13.

2 Fold the body in half. Fold the base of the tail into the hips. Fold up the wings. **Ⓐ**

3 Pull up the neck and turn it over. **Ⓑ**

4 Fold the head over the top of the neck. **Ⓒ**

5 Fold the base of the bill into the head. **Ⓓ Ⓔ**

6 Roll the two halves of the hips over a dowel. Then cross the tabs of the interlocking joint under the tail. **Ⓕ**

7 Shape the wings following the scored folding lines in them. **Ⓖ**

8 Color your Goose by referencing the project photos. The goose depicted in the photos was colored after the Canada goose. You may experiment with your own coloring and turn your bird into a different kind of goose if you would like.

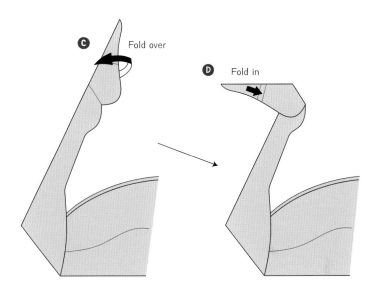

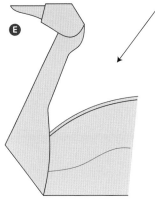

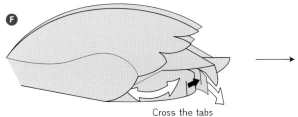

Cross the tabs

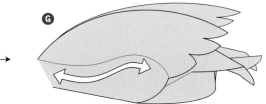

Canary

Canaries were first domesticated in the 1600s. Their sensitivity to toxic gases made them a useful warning system for coal miners right up until the late 1980s.

1 Using the Canary templates on page 96, score the folding lines, then cut along all the solid lines, including the eyes, the beak, the internal cuts of the wings, and the cuts for interlocking joints, as depicted in How to Use This Book on pages 5-13.

2 Fold the body in half using the scored centerline as a guide. Pull down the head while you fold the back of the head over the neck. **Ⓐ**

3 Push up the bottom halves of the beak. Push in the cheeks to shape them. Roll the two halves of the neck over a dowel to round them. **Ⓑ**

4 Cross the tabs of the neck joint. **Ⓒ**

5 Apply a small amount of glue to the outside of the tab of the beak. Fold it down and attach it to the inside of the other half of the beak. **Ⓓ Ⓔ**

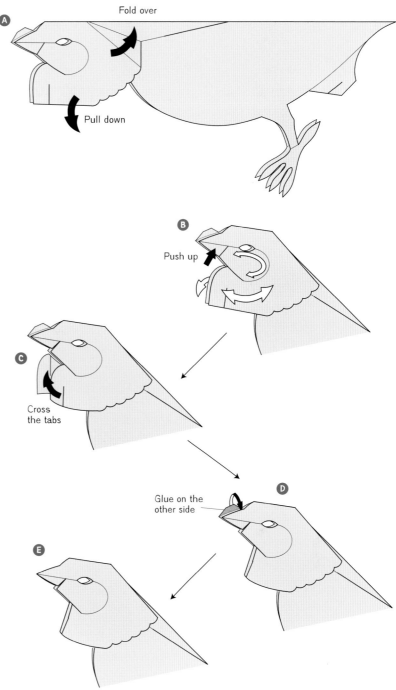

Ⓐ Fold over
Pull down

Ⓑ Push up

Ⓒ Cross the tabs

Ⓓ Glue on the other side

Ⓔ

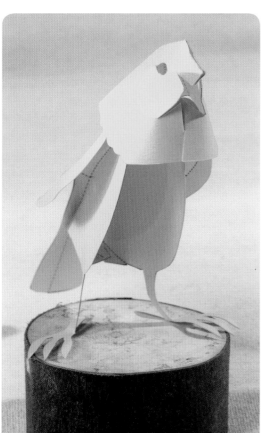

Tip

Instead of using white cardstock and adding color, you can make this bird with a sheet of yellow cardstock.

6 Fold in the tabs of the interlocking joint at the bottom of the body. Cross the tabs. **F**

7 Fold the feet out to the sides at a right angle. **G**

8 Shape the feathers of the wings following the scored folding lines. Pull down the tail while you squeeze in its base. **H** **I**

9 Attach the wings to the body by sliding the front end of the wings under the cut on the back and running the tail end of the body through the cut in the tail. Roll the feet over a dowel. **J**

10 Adjust the angle of the legs and feet so that your Canary will stand securely on the ground.

11 If you didn't use yellow cardstock, add color to your Canary by referencing the project photos.

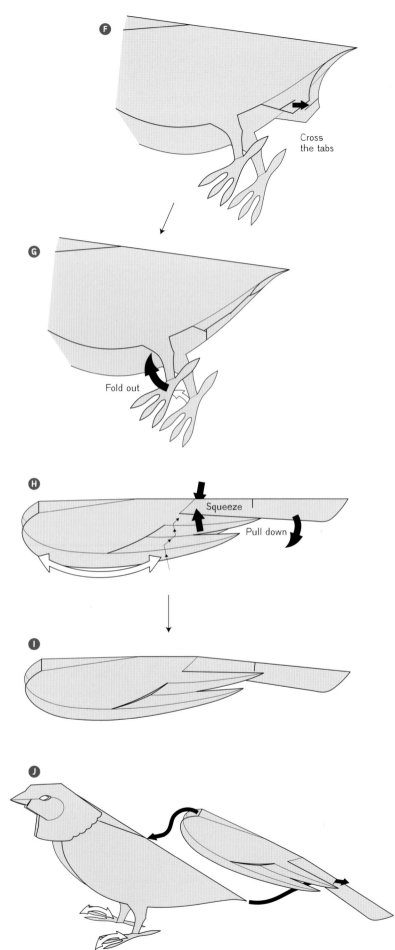

Crow

Considered one of the world's most intelligent animals, crows appear to be able to count, make and use tools, and even recognize individual humans by distinguishing faces!

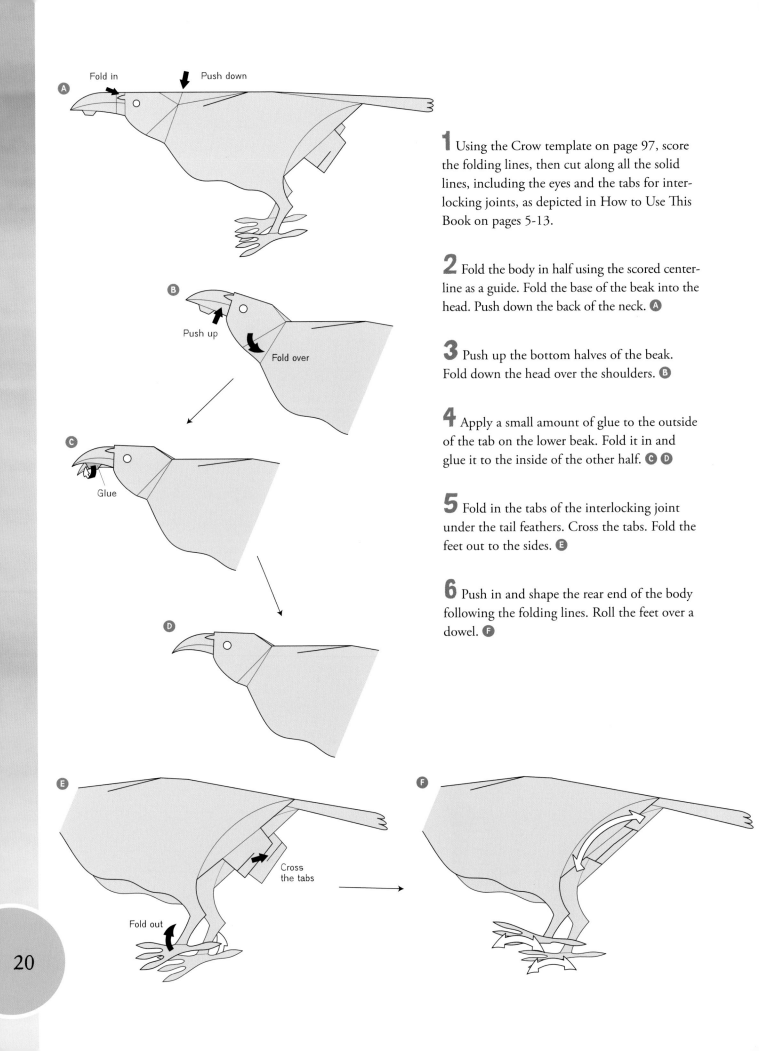

1 Using the Crow template on page 97, score the folding lines, then cut along all the solid lines, including the eyes and the tabs for interlocking joints, as depicted in How to Use This Book on pages 5–13.

2 Fold the body in half using the scored centerline as a guide. Fold the base of the beak into the head. Push down the back of the neck. **A**

3 Push up the bottom halves of the beak. Fold down the head over the shoulders. **B**

4 Apply a small amount of glue to the outside of the tab on the lower beak. Fold it in and glue it to the inside of the other half. **C D**

5 Fold in the tabs of the interlocking joint under the tail feathers. Cross the tabs. Fold the feet out to the sides. **E**

6 Push in and shape the rear end of the body following the folding lines. Roll the feet over a dowel. **F**

Fold in   Push down

Push up   Fold over

Glue

Cross the tabs

Fold out

20

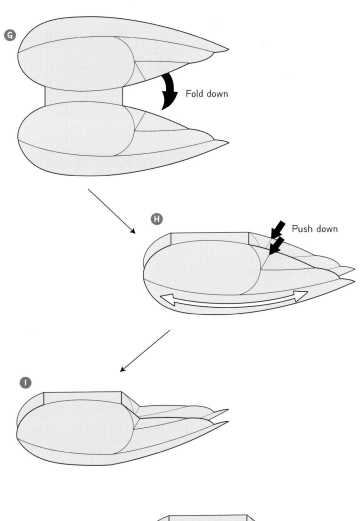

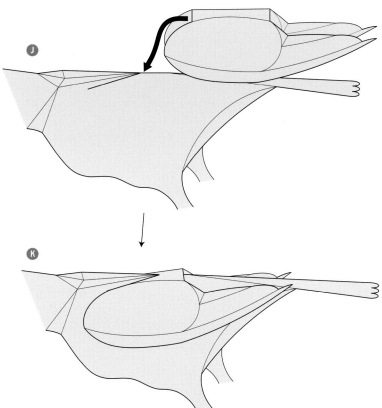

7 Fold down the wings in half. **G**

8 Shape the wings following the scored folding lines. **H** **I**

9 Attach the wings to the body by sliding the front end of the wings under the cut on the back. **J** **K**

10 Adjust the angle of the legs so that your Crow will stand securely on the ground.

11 Color your Crow any way you would like.

Tip

You can make your Crow with a sheet of black or dark navy blue cardstock and skip the coloring step.

21

Quail

The Quail inhabits woodlands and forests around the world. It has a teardrop-shaped, forward-drooping plume on top of its head, which consists of six overlaying feathers.

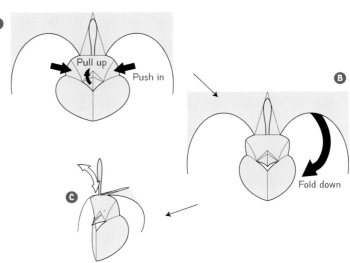

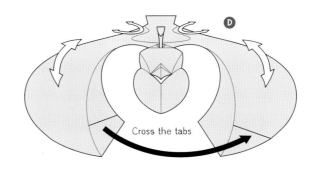

1 Using the Quail template on page 98, score the folding lines, then cut along all the solid lines, including the beak, the plume on top of the head, and the tabs for an interlocking joint, as depicted in How to Use This Book on pages 5-13.

2 Push in the sides of the head, pull up the beak, and pocket fold its base into the head. Ⓐ

3 Fold down the neck behind the head. Ⓑ

4 Roll the head plume over a dowel to curl it. Ⓒ

5 Shape the back and the sides of the body as illustrated. Bring the two halves of the chest into the center and cross the tabs for the interlocking joint. Ⓓ

6 Push in the top of the chest. Ⓔ Ⓕ

7 Add color to your Quail by referencing the project photos.

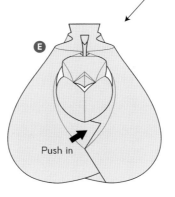

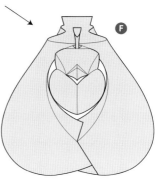

Kiwi

The Kiwi is a shy, flightless bird and a national symbol of New Zealand. Kiwifruit, originally imported to New Zealand from China as the Chinese gooseberry, was renamed for its resemblance to the Kiwi.

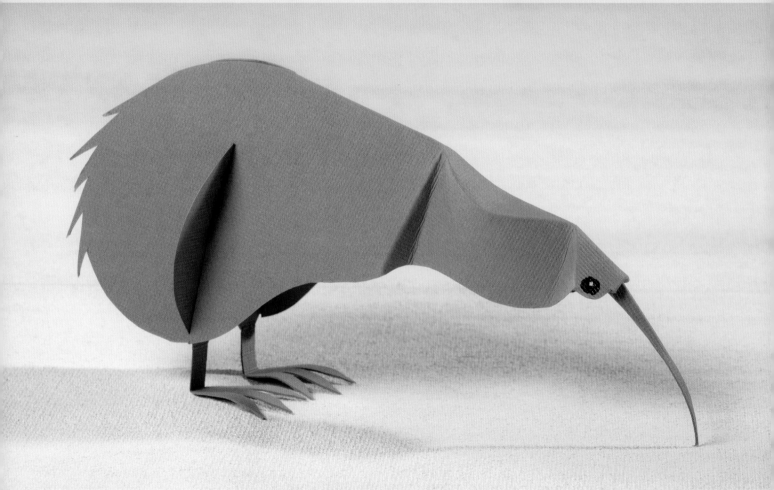

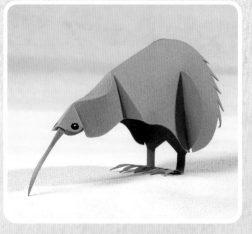
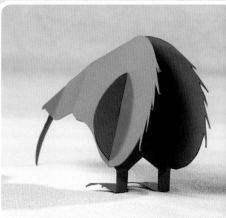

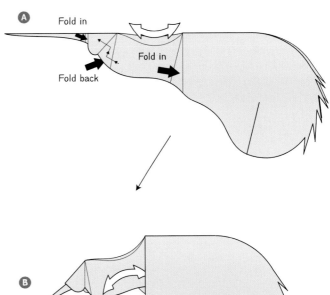

1 Using the Kiwi templates on page 98, score the folding lines, then cut along all the solid lines, including the cuts for an interlocking joint, as depicted in How to Use This Book on pages 5-13.

2 Fold the body in half following the scored centerline. Fold in the base of the beak into the head. Fold back the head over the neck. Push down the back of the neck. Ⓐ

3 Roll the beak over a dowel to add a curve to it. Shape the neck by pushing in its sides. Ⓑ

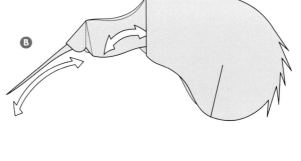

4 Fold the feet out at right angles. Ⓒ

5 Cross the cuts at the bottom of the body and the ones at the top of the legs. Roll the feet over a dowel. Ⓓ

6 Add color to your Kiwi by referencing the project photos.

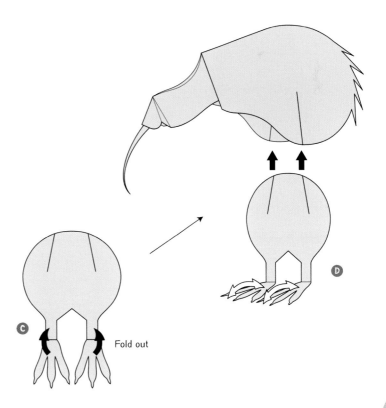

Penguin

The Antarctic environment where many Penguins live can be brutally cold. Happily, the bird's thick sub-dermal fat and its densely packed feathers allow the penguin to survive comfortably.

1 Using the Penguin templates on page 99, score the folding lines, then cut along all the solid lines, including the tabs for interlocking joints, as depicted in How to Use This Book on pages 5-13.

2 Fold the template of the Penguin's back in half using the scored centerline as a guide. Pull down the head. Pocket fold the tail into the hips. **A**

3 Roll the beak over a dowel. **B**

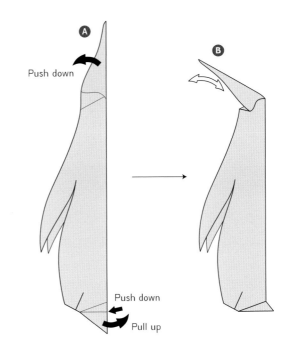

4 Fold the template of the Penguin's stomach in half using the scored centerline as a guide. Push in the center at the bottom, turning over the feet. **C**

5 Fold the feet out to the front. **D**

6 Fold down the toes. **E**

7 Attach the two templates by crossing the cuts at the bottom of the back template and the ones at the back of the stomach template. **F**

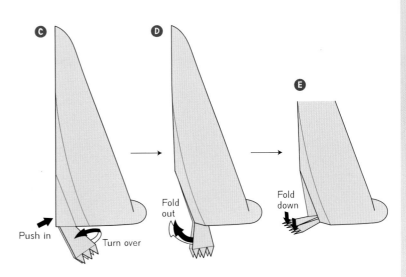

8 Add color to your Penguin by referencing the project photos. The penguins in this book were colored after the emperor penguins. Of course, you can color yours differently for a different type of penguin.

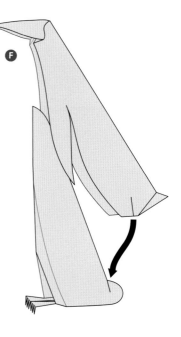

Penguin Chick

To make this FREE bonus project, go to www.larkcrafts.com/bonus for instructions and templates.

Swan

The feathers of swans in the Northern Hemisphere are almost entirely white, but those in the Southern Hemisphere have at least some black feathers.

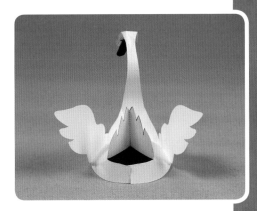

1 Using the Swan template on page 100, score the folding lines, then cut along all the solid lines, including the cut on the head and the tabs for an interlocking joint, as depicted in How to Use This Book on pages 5-13.

2 Fold the wings over the back. Ⓐ

3 Fold the body in half. Fold up the neck from the shoulders following the scored folding lines. When you do this, the front edges of the wings should be tucked in behind the shoulders. Ⓑ Ⓒ

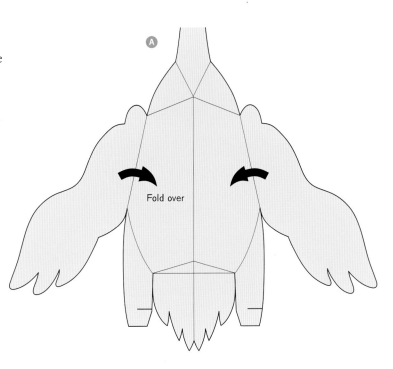

Ⓐ

Fold over

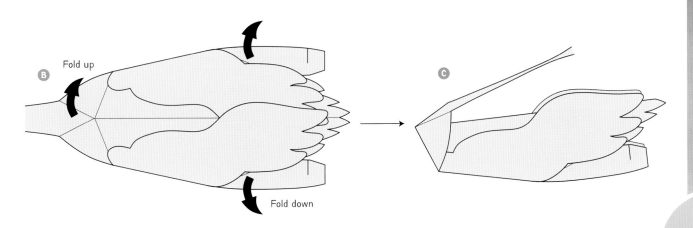

Ⓑ Fold up

Ⓒ

Fold down

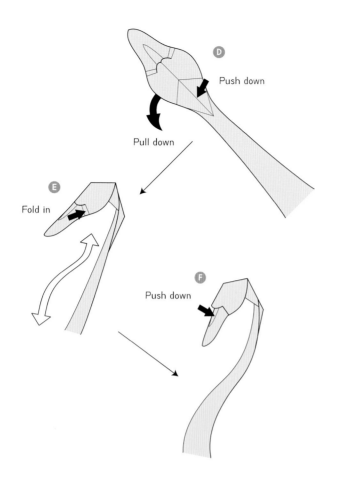

Push down

Pull down

Fold in

Push down

4 Fold the head in half and pull it down while you push down and valley fold the top of the head. **D**

5 Fold the base of the bill into the head. Roll the neck over a dowel and shape it to your liking. **E**

6 Push down and flatten the bridge of the bill. **F**

7 Pull up the tail and pocket fold its base into the hips. **G**

8 Roll the two halves of the hips over a dowel. Then cross the tabs of the interlocking joint under the tail. **H** **I**

9 Add color to your Swan by referencing the project photos.

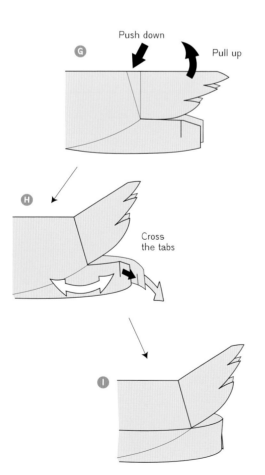

Push down

Pull up

Cross the tabs

Toucan

The Toucan's most outstanding feature, its colorful large bill, is a lightweight honeycomb structure of bone material that contains a lot of air.

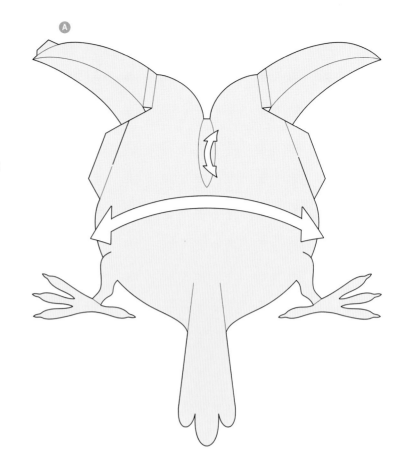

1 Using the Toucan template on page 101, score the folding lines, then cut along all the solid lines including the tabs for an interlocking joint, as depicted in How to Use This Book on pages 5-13.

2 Roll the template over the edge of a table to round the body. Push down the oval shape in the middle of the template. Ⓐ

3 Bring the two halves of the head together. Fold the base of the beak into the head. Ⓑ

4 Push up the bottom half of the beak following the scored folding lines in the middle. Ⓒ

5 Apply a small amount of glue to the outside of the tab on the beak. Fold it in and glue it to the inside of the other half of the beak. Ⓓ

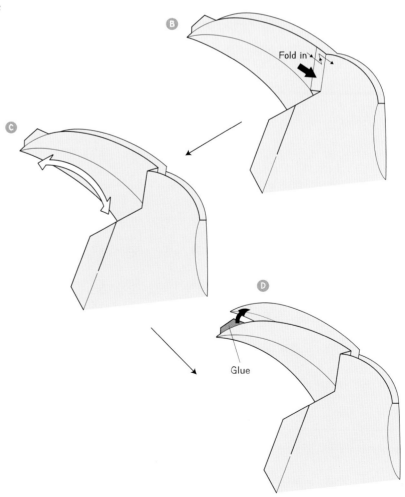

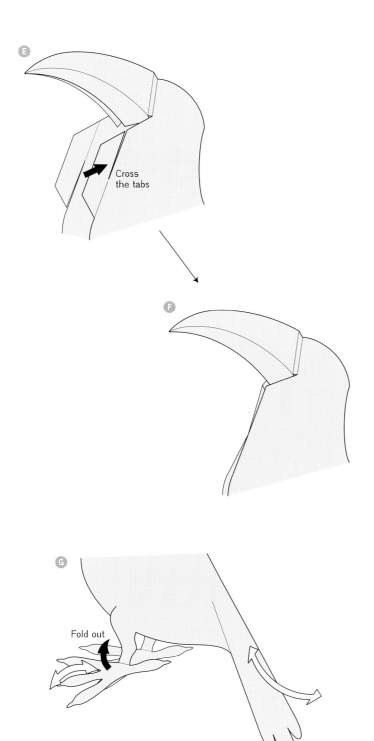

Cross
the tabs

6 Cross the tabs of the chest joint. E F

7 Fold out the feet. Roll them over a dowel. Roll the tail over a dowel, too. G

8 Add color to your Toucan by referencing the project photos.

Fold out

Flamingo

Flamingos are born with grayish white plumage. It takes about two years for the bird's diet, which consists of brine shrimp and blue-green algae, to turn the Flamingo's feathers that famous pink.

1 Using the Flamingo templates on pages 102 and 103, score the folding lines, then cut along all the solid lines, including the cut for the wing connection on the back and the tabs for the interlocking joints, as depicted in How to Use This Book on pages 5-13.

2 Fold the base of the bill into the head. Fold the head over the top of the neck. **A**

3 Apply a small amount of glue to the outside of the tab on the bill. Fold it in and glue the two halves of the bill together. **B**

4 Shape the bill by pushing up the bottom half of it following the scored folding lines. **C**

5 Pull up the neck while you pocket fold its bottom into the shoulders. Push down and turn over the tail. **D**

6 Roll the neck over a dowel to create a curve to your liking. **E**

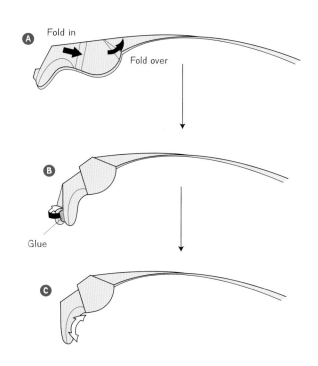

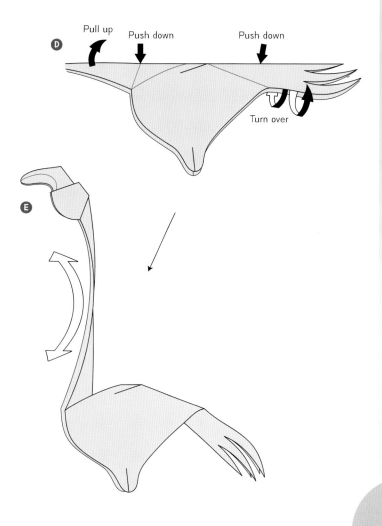

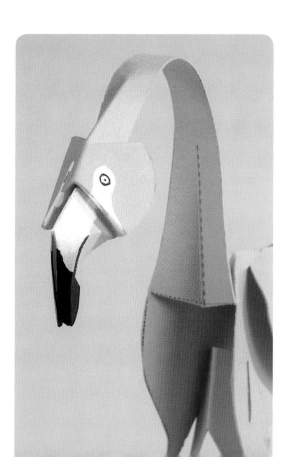

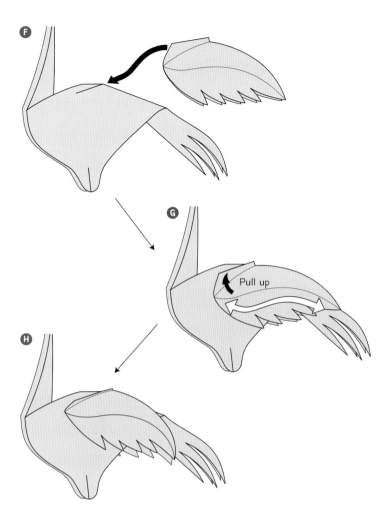

7 Fold the wings in half. Connect the wings to the body by sliding the front end of the wings under the cut on the back. **F**

8 Shape the wings following the folding lines. Pull up the wings toward the shoulders. **G** **H**

9 There are two different designs of the legs: one with both feet on the ground, the other with one leg up. I am going to discuss the second design here. Squeeze the legs in half, paying attention to the different folds between the two. The bent leg requires valley folds and the straight leg requires peak folds. **I**

10 Fold back the right leg from the hips. Fold up the lower leg from the knee. Fold back the foot from the ankle. All you need to do about the left leg is to fold up the foot. **J**

11 Bring the two legs together. Wedge the left shin into the cut of the right ankle. **K** **L**

12 If you decide to make your Flamingo with both legs on the ground, use the other leg template and repeat the same straight leg folding for both legs.

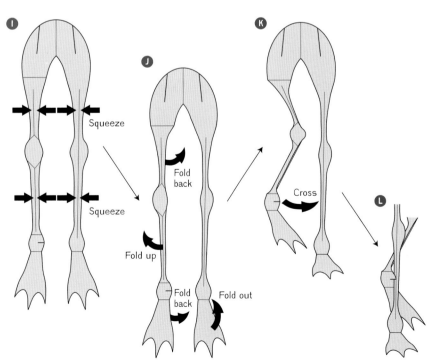

13 Attach the legs to the body by crossing the cuts at the bottom of the body and the ones at the top of the legs. Ⓜ Ⓝ

14 Add color to your Flamingo by referencing the project photos.

15 To display the bird, you will need a display stand. A possible design is discussed in Display Methods on pages 12-13. See the illustration of the Crowned Crane for reference.

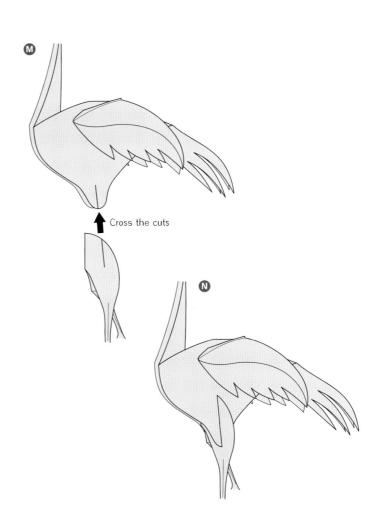

Cross the cuts

Frigatebird

The Frigatebird's most striking feature is a large red gular sac under the male's bill, which the bird inflates during the breeding season to attract females.

1 Using the Frigatebird templates on page 104, score the folding lines, then cut along all the solid lines, including the cut in the body for the wing joint, the internal cuts of the wings, and the tabs for interlocking joints, as depicted in How to Use This Book on pages 5-13.

2 Fold the body in half. Fold in the base of the beak into the head. Fold down the tip of the beak. **A**

3 Roll the two halves of the gular sac over a dowel to round them. Cross the tabs of the interlocking joint to connect them. **B**

4 Pull down the gular sac to lower the head. **C D**

5 Pull up the tabs of the interlocking wing joints, and cross the tabs with the bases of the wings. Shape the wings following the scored folding lines. **E**

6 Attach the wings to the body by sliding the front end of the wings under the cut on the back and running the tail end of the body through the cut in the tail. **F**

7 Add color to your Frigatebird by referencing the project photos.

8 You can hang your Frigatebird by a thread for display. Run the thread through the spot marked X.

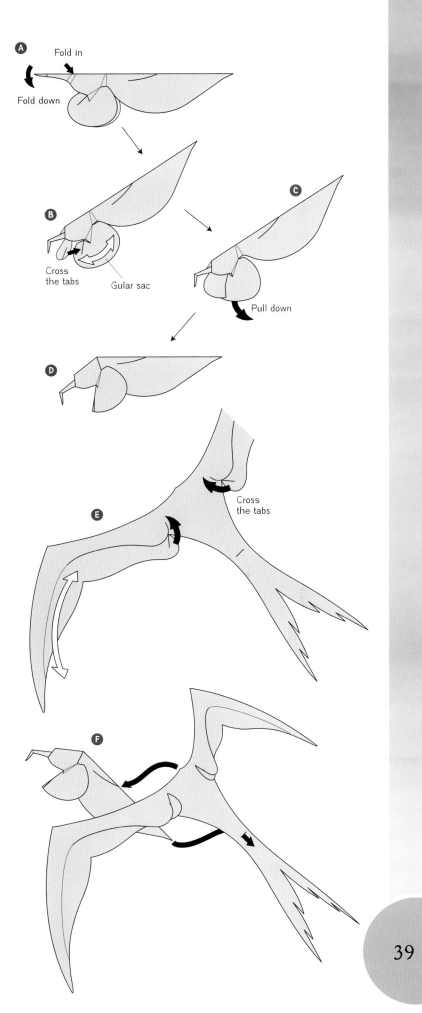

Great Horned Owl

One of the Great Horned Owl's most striking features is its large eyes, which are almost as big as human eyes. Its spectacular binocular vision allows it to see prey in low light.

Owlet

To make this FREE bonus project, go to www.larkcrafts.com/bonus for instructions and templates.

1 Using the Great Horned Owl template on page 105, score the folding lines, then cut along all the solid lines, including the beak and the cuts for interlocking joints, as depicted in How to Use This Book on pages 5-13.

2 Fold the body in half using the scored centerline as a guide. Pull down the head, push down the back of the neck, and fold the base of the tail into the hips. Ⓐ Ⓑ

3 Fold up the beak. Cross the tabs of the interlocking joint at the bottom of the head. Ⓒ Ⓓ

4 Push in the cheeks following the scored folding lines. Roll the feathers on both sides of the head to add curves to them. Ⓔ

5 Roll the two halves of the body over a dowel. Bring the tabs of the interlocking chest joint together and cross the tabs. Fold the feet out. Roll them over a dowel. Ⓕ Ⓖ

6 Adjust the angle of the legs so that your Great Horned Owl will stand securely on the ground. The tail of the Owl is meant to hang lower than the feet. Add color to your Great Horned Owl by referencing the project photo. Place the bird on a base to display it.

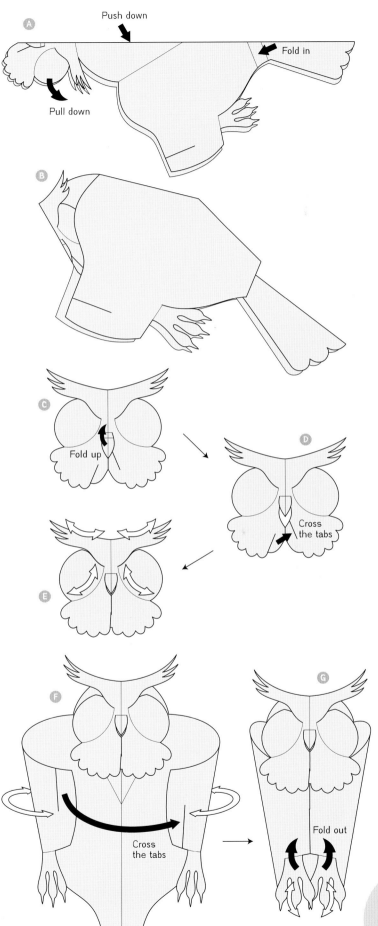

41

Kingfisher

Perched on a tree branch or a rock close to water, the Kingfisher carefully searches for small fish with its piercing eyes. The shaggy crest on the Belted Kingfisher's head gives it a royal air.

1 Using the Kingfisher template on page 106, score the folding lines, then cut along all the solid lines, including the lines under the eyes, the beak, the internal cuts of the wings, and the tabs for the interlocking joints, as depicted in How to Use This Book on pages 5-13.

2 Fold the body in half using the scored centerline in the middle of the head as a guide. Fold the beak up at a right angle and over the face. Fold down the wings to the sides. **A**

3 Fold the head down and over the neck. Shape the wings by following the scored folding lines. **B**

4 Push up the bottom half of the beak. Cross the tabs of the chest joint. **C**

5 Fold the feet out to the sides. Fold down the tabs of the tail joint. **D**

6 Cross the tabs of the tail joint. **E** **F**

7 Add color to your Kingfisher by referencing the project photos. Place it on a low base to display.

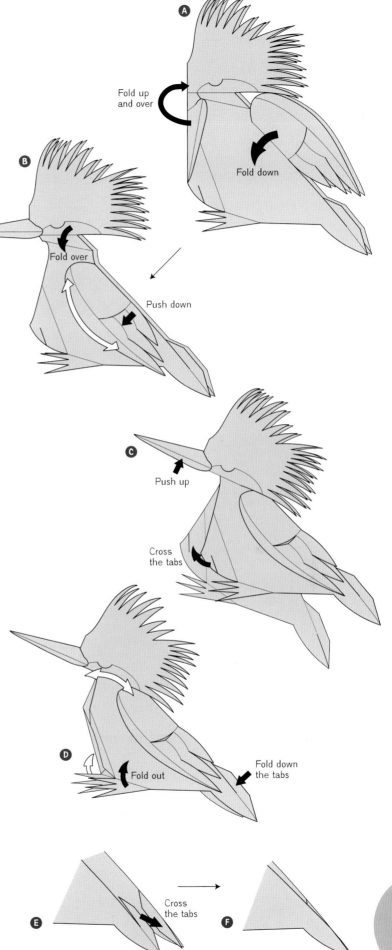

Hummingbird

Hummingbirds are the smallest birds in the world with the tiniest ones weighing less than a penny. Their wings beat at speeds of up to 80 times per second!

1 Using the Hummingbird templates on page 106, score the folding lines, then cut along all the solid lines, including the cut in the body for the wing joint, as depicted in How to Use This Book on pages 5-13.

2 Fold the body in half. Roll the body over a dowel to add roundness to it. Apply a small amount of glue to the inside of the beak and glue the beak together. **A**

3 Shape the wings by following the scored folding lines in them. Roll the tail over a dowel. **B**

4 Attach the wings to the body by sliding the front end of the wings under the cut on the back and running the tip of the tail end of the body through the cut in the tail. **C**

5 Add color to your Hummingbird by referencing the project photos. The Hummingbirds shown were made with metallic vellum paper and colored with metallic paint.

6 You can hang the Hummingbird by a thread for display. Run the thread through the spot marked X.

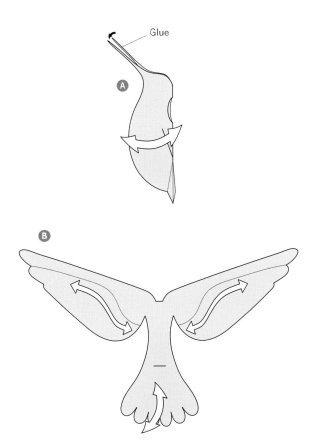

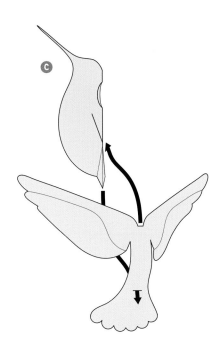

Pelican

The Pelican is famous for its long beak and large throat pouch, which the bird uses just like a fishing net to catch prey.

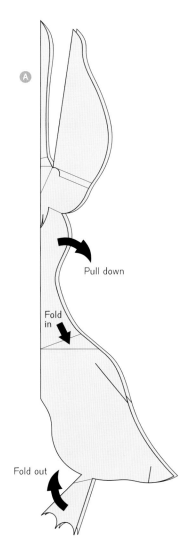

1 Using the Pelican templates on page 107, score the folding lines, then cut along all the solid lines, including the lines under the eyes, the feathers at the top of the head, and the tabs for interlocking joints, as depicted in How to Use This Book on pages 5-13.

2 Fold the template in half using the scored centerline as a guide. Pull down the neck toward the back while you pocket fold the bottom of the neck into the shoulders. Fold the feet out. A

3 Turn over the head and bring it up front. B

4 Fold the bases of the upper and lower bills into the head. C

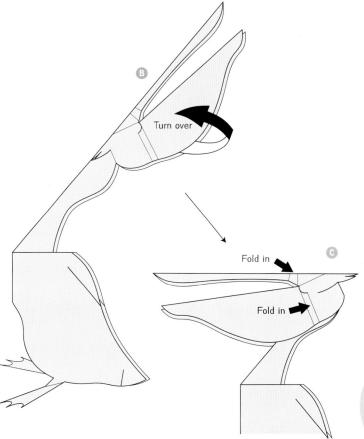

47

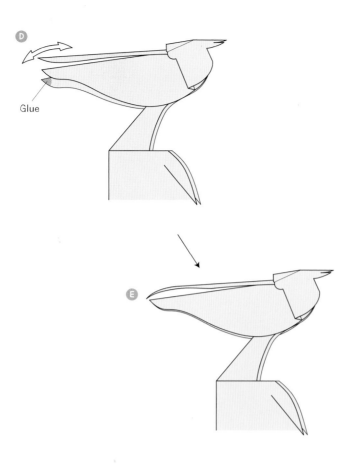

Glue

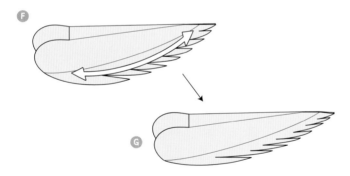

5 Apply a small amount of glue to the tip of the lower bill on one side, and glue the two halves together. Roll the tip of the upper bill over a dowel. **D** **E**

6 Fold the wings in half. Shape the wings following the scored folding lines. **F** **G**

7 Roll the two halves of the hips over a dowel. Cross the tabs of the interlocking joint. **H**

8 Attach the wings by sliding the front end under the cuts on the back. **I**

9 Add color to your Pelican by referencing the project photos.

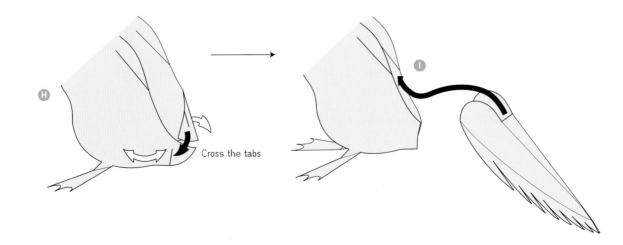

Cross the tabs

Roadrunner

The roadrunner got its name from the fact that it's often seen racing down the road in front of oncoming vehicles. It can run at speeds of 20 to 26 mph.

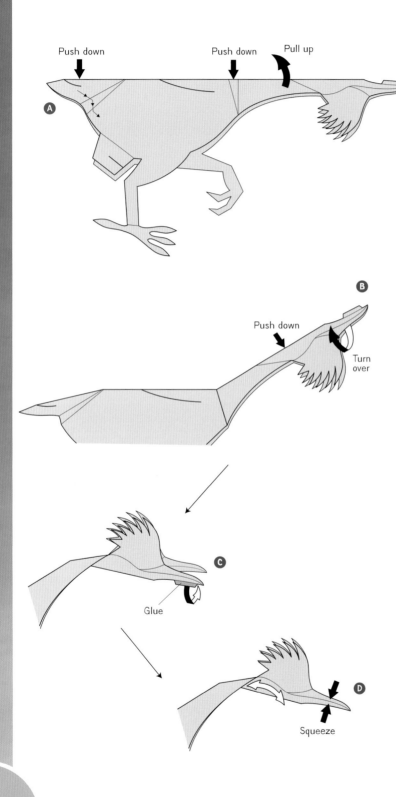

Push down   Push down   Pull up

Push down   Turn over

Glue

Squeeze

1 Using the Roadrunner templates on page 108, score the folding lines, then cut along all the solid lines, including the cuts for the wing joint on the back and the tabs for an inter-locking joint, as depicted in How to Use This Book on pages 5-13.

2 Fold the template in half using the scored centerline as a guide. Pull up the neck. Pocket fold the bottom of the neck into the shoulders. Push down the tail end of the body. **A**

3 Push down the head and turn it over. **B**

4 Apply a small amount of glue to the outside of the tab on the beak. Fold it in and glue it to the inside of the other half of the beak. **C**

5 Squeeze the beak to shape it. Push up the jaw line using the scored folding lines as a guide. **D**

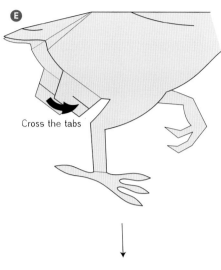

Cross the tabs

6 Fold in the tabs of the interlocking joint at the bottom of the body. Cross the tabs. **E**

7 Fold the right foot out to the side. **F**

8 Fold the wings in half. Shape them following the scored folding lines. **G**

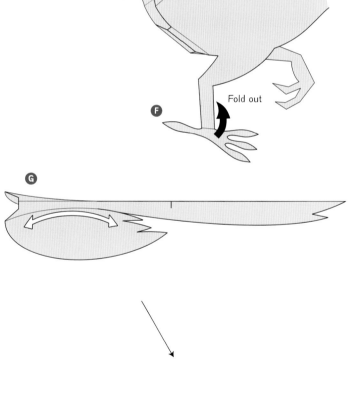

Fold out

9 Attach the wings to the body by sliding the front end of the wings under the cut on the back and running the tail end of the body through the cut in the base of the tail. Roll the feet over a dowel. **H**

10 Add color to your Roadrunner by referencing the project photos.

11 To display the bird, you will need a stand. One possible design is discussed in Display Methods on pages 12 and 13.

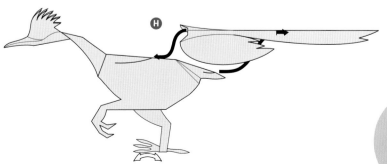

Swallow

Swallows are brave enough to live very close to humans, often building their nests in urban environments such as the underside of a roof, a bridge, or freeway overpass.

1 Using the Swallow templates on page 109, score the folding lines, then cut along all the solid lines, including the cut in the body for the wing joint, the opening on the back of the neck, the internal cuts of the wings, and the tabs for interlocking joints, as depicted in How to Use This Book on pages 5-13.

2 Fold the body in half. Apply a small amount of glue to the inside of the tip of the beak. Glue the two halves of the beak together. Push up the bottom half of the head following the scored folding lines. **A B**

3 Pull up the tabs of the interlocking wing joints. Cross the tabs with the bases of the wings. Shape the wings following their scored folding lines. **C D**

4 Attach the wings to the body by sliding the front end of the wings under the cut on the back and running the tail end of the body through the cut in the tail. Squeeze the base of the tail. **E**

5 Add color to your Swallow by referencing the project photos.

6 You can hang the bird by a thread for display. Run the thread through the spot marked X.

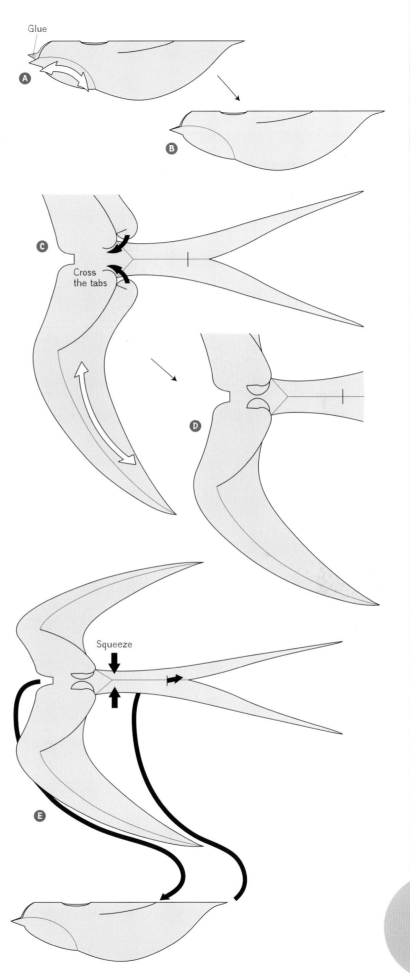

Dove

The Dove's relationship with humans goes back thousands of years. They play integral roles in many religions. Even today, doves are released as a symbolic gesture in ceremonies such as weddings and funerals.

1 Using the Dove templates on page 110, score the folding lines, then cut along all the solid lines, including the eyes, the cut in the body for the wing joint, the internal cuts of the wings, and the tabs for interlocking joints, as depicted in How to Use This Book on pages 5-13.

2 Fold the body in half. Fold the head over the top of the neck. Apply a small amount of glue on the inside of one half of the beak and glue the two halves together. **Ⓐ**

3 Shape the tail end of the body following the folding lines. **Ⓑ**

4 Pull up the tabs of the interlocking wing joints and cross the tabs with the bases of the wings. Shape the wings following the scored folding lines in them. **Ⓒ**

5 Attach the wings to the body by sliding the front end of the wings under the cut on the back and running the tail end of the body through the cut in the tail. **Ⓓ**

6 Color your Dove by referencing the project photos.

7 You can hang the Dove by a thread for display. Run the thread through the spot marked X.

Dodo

The Dodo was a large flightless bird that lived peacefully on the island of Mauritius until Dutch sailors discovered the bird in the late 1500s. Seventy years later, not a single Dodo remained.

1 Using the Dodo templates on page 111, score the folding lines, then cut along all the solid lines, including the cuts in the body for the wing joint and the tabs for interlocking joints, as depicted in How to Use This Book on pages 5-13.

2 Fold in the top of the forehead under the head. Ⓐ

3 Pull down the two halves of the neck to the center. Ⓑ

4 Pull up the nose. Fold down the beak. Push in and shape the cheeks following the folding lines. Apply a small amount of glue to the tab on the neck, fold it in, and glue it to the inside of the other half of the neck. Ⓒ

5 Valley fold the tail in half and fold down the entire tail. Ⓓ

6 Run the wings from inside through the cuts in the body. Add curves to the center of the body following the folding lines across the torso. Ⓔ

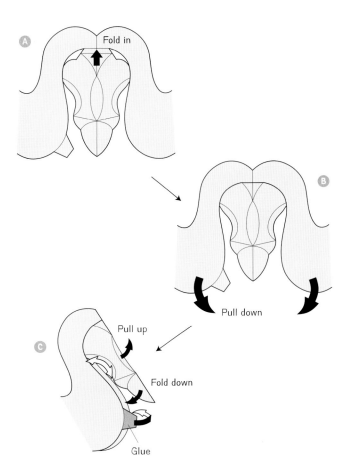

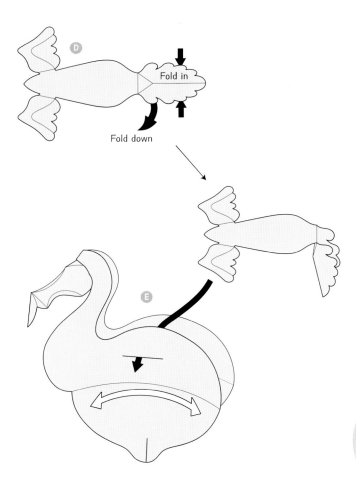

57

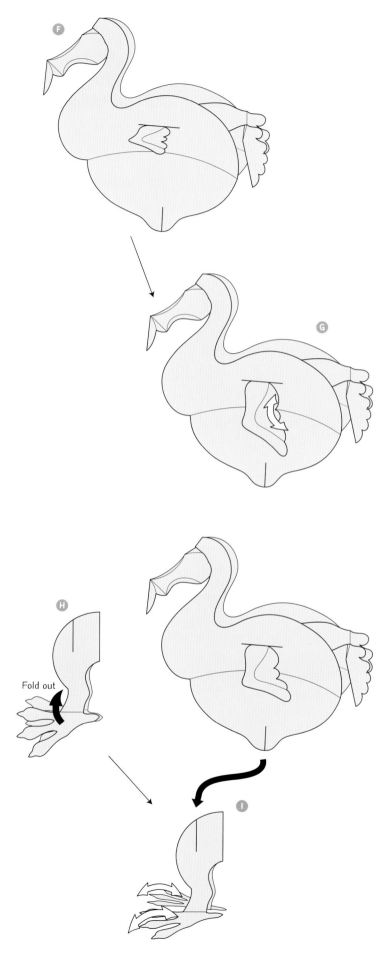

7 Fold down the wings to the sides of the body and shape them according to their folding lines. **F** **G**

8 Fold the legs in half. Fold the feet out to the sides. **H**

9 Cross the cuts at the top of the legs and the ones at the bottom of the body and connect the legs to the body. Roll the feet over a dowel. **I**

10 Adjust the angle of the legs so that your Dodo will stand securely on the ground.

11 Add color to your Dodo by referencing the project photos. The Dodo is extinct, but he will live forever in your home.

Fold out

58

Blue-Footed Booby

The male Blue-Footed Booby's courtship dance involves strutting, showing off nest materials he's gathered, pointing his bill and wings to the sky, and then a final display of his beautiful bright blue feet.

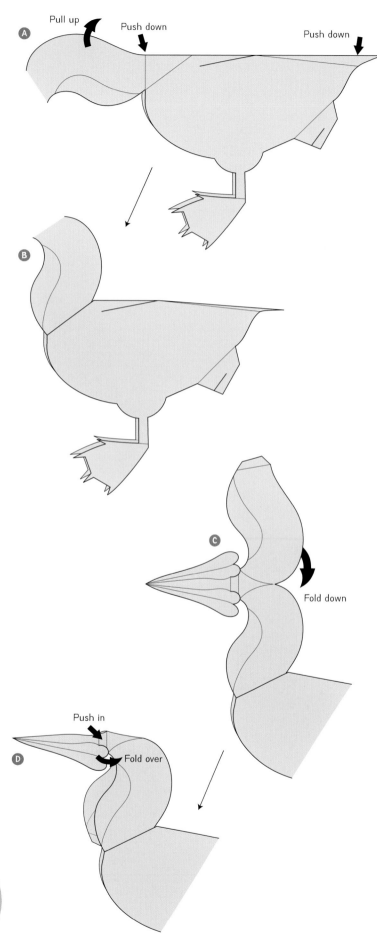

1 Using the Blue-Footed Booby templates on page 112, score the folding lines, then cut along all the solid lines, including the lines around the eyes and the cuts for interlocking joints, as depicted in How to Use This Book on pages 5-13.

2 Fold the body in half using the scored centerline as a guide. Pull up the neck while you pocket fold the bottom of the neck into the shoulders. Push down the tail end of the body. Ⓐ Ⓑ

3 Fold the head and neck in half. Ⓒ

4 Push in the base of the beak and make the sides of the beak go over the cheeks. Ⓓ

5 Push up the bottom halves of the beak. Shape the front side of the neck following the scored folding lines. **E**

6 Bring the bottom of the neck not connected to the body in between the shoulders. **F**

7 Apply a small amount of glue to the outside of the tab as shown in the illustration. Fold up the tab and attach the glued side to the bottom of the neck you pocket folded earlier. **G** **H**

8 Fold in the tabs of the interlocking joint at the rear end of the body. Cross the tabs. **I**

9 Fold the feet out to the sides at a right angle. **J**

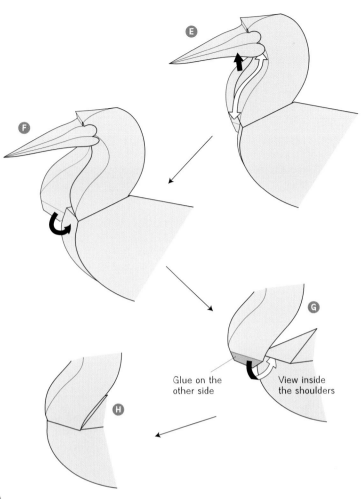

Glue on the other side

View inside the shoulders

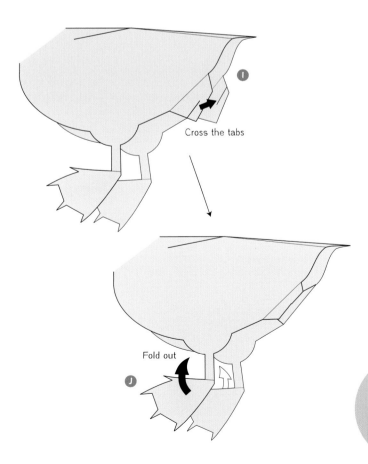

Cross the tabs

Fold out

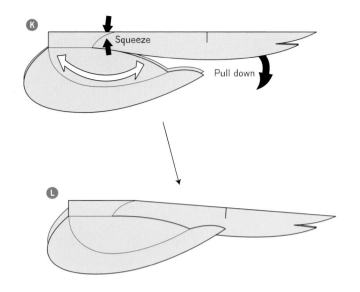

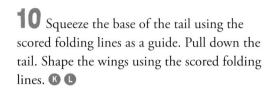

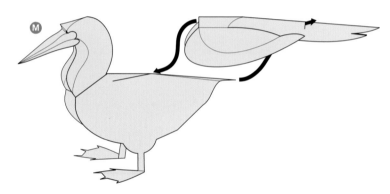

10 Squeeze the base of the tail using the scored folding lines as a guide. Pull down the tail. Shape the wings using the scored folding lines. **K** **L**

11 Attach the wings to the body by sliding the front end of the wings under the cut on the back and running the tail end of the body through the cut in the tail. **M**

12 Adjust the angle of the legs so that your Blue-Footed Booby will stand securely on the ground.

13 Add color to your Blue-Footed Booby by referencing the project photos.

Falcon

Falcons are the fastest animal on earth and can dive in excess of 200 miles an hour. The art of falconry-hunting with trained falcons-is thought to have started in 2000 B.C. in Mesopotamia.

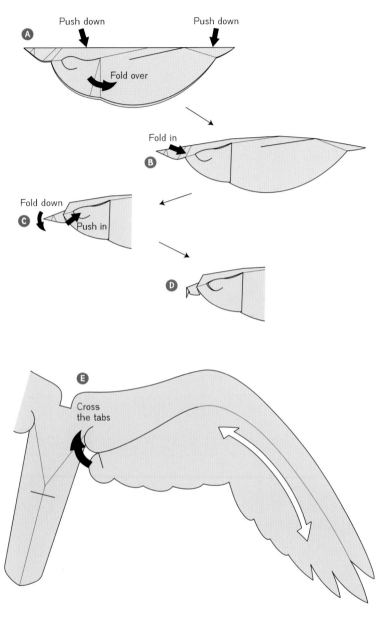

1 Using the Falcon templates on page 113, score the folding lines, then cut along all the solid lines, including the line around the eyes, the cuts for the wing connection on the back, and the tabs for the interlocking joints, as depicted in How to Use This Book on pages 5-13.

2 Fold the body in half following the scored centerline. Push down the top of the head and fold the neck over the shoulders. Push down the tail end of the body. **A**

3 Fold in the base of the beak under the eyes. **B**

4 Fold down the tip of the beak. Push the eyes back into the sockets. **C D**

5 Pull up the tabs of the interlocking wing joints and cross the tabs with the bases of the wings. Shape the wings following the scored folding lines in them. **E**

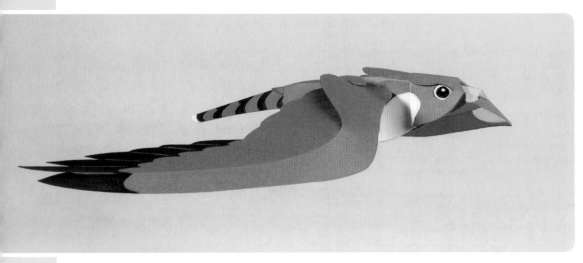

6 Fold down the tail from the scored folding lines. **F**

7 Attach the wings to the body by sliding the front end of the wings under the cut on the back and running the tail end of the body through the cut in the tail. **G**

8 Add color to your Falcon by referencing the project photos.

9 If you want to display your Falcon flying, run the thread through the X marked on the back of the body.

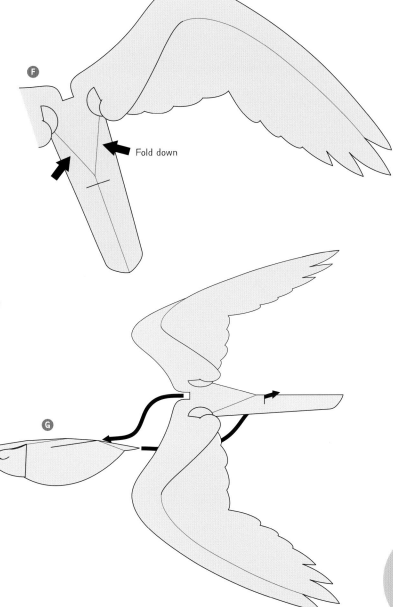

F

Fold down

G

Parakeet

Parakeets are very intelligent birds. They can mimic sounds, learn words, and sing. A parakeet named Puck holds the world record for the largest vocabulary at 1,728 words.

1 Using the Parakeet templates on pages 114 and 115, score the folding lines, then cut along all the solid lines, including the cuts for the wing joint, the cuts around the eyes and cheeks, the beak, the internal lines of the wings, and the tabs for interlocking joints, as depicted in How to Use This Book on pages 5-13.

2 Fold the body in half using the scored centerline as a guide. Pull down the neck while you pocket fold the bottom of the neck into the shoulders. **Ⓐ**

3 Pull down the head while you valley fold its top. **Ⓑ**

4 Unfold and open up the head a little. **Ⓒ**

5 Pull up the nostrils. Push up the beak. **Ⓓ**

6 Bring the two halves of the jaw together and cross the tabs. **Ⓔ**

7 Push in the sides of the head. Roll the neck over a dowel. **Ⓕ**

8 Roll the cheeks over a dowel. **Ⓖ**

Tip

Parakeets are very colorful birds. To make your Parakeet, start with cardstock in a dominant color for the particular bird you want to make and add patches of other colors later on.

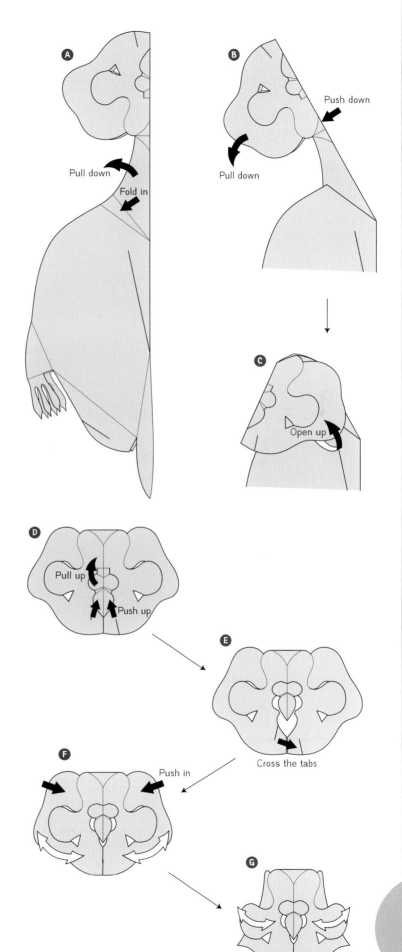

67

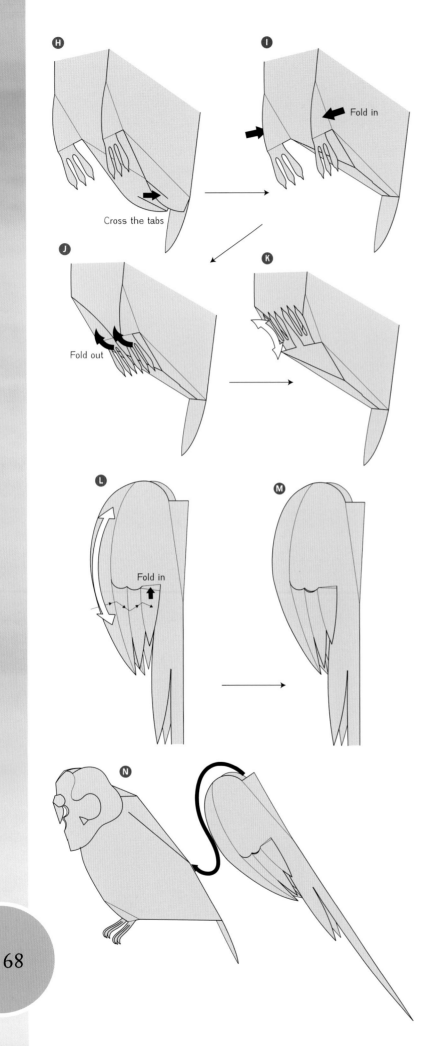

9 Fold in the tabs of the joint at the bottom of the body and cross them. **H**

10 Fold the feet in toward the center of the body. **I**

11 Fold the feet out to the front. **J**

12 Roll the feet over a dowel. **K**

13 Fold the wings in half and shape them following the up-and-down patterns of the feathers. Fold in the shortest feathers as illustrated. **L M**

14 Attach the wings to the body by sliding the front end of the wings under the cut on the back. **N**

15 Adjust the angle of the legs so that your Parakeet will stand comfortably on the ground. The long tail of the Parakeet is meant to hang lower than the feet. Display the bird on a base or on a tree branch.

16 Add color to your Parakeet by referencing the project photos.

68

Pheasant

The Common Pheasant is actually native to China.
One of the most popular game birds, a pheasant will
fly for a short distance if startled, but prefers running.

1 Using the Pheasant templates on page 116, score the folding lines, then cut along all the solid lines, including the cuts for the wing joint on the back, the crest, and the tabs for interlocking joints, as depicted in How to Use This Book on pages 5-13.

2 Fold the template in half using the scored centerline as a guide. Pull up the neck. Pocket fold the bottom of the neck into the shoulders. Push down the tail end of the body. **A**

3 Fold the head down and over the top of the neck. Fold the base of the beak into the head. **B**

4 Push up the bottom half of the beak. Roll the crest on the head over a dowel to add a curve to it. **C**

5 Shape the cheeks as illustrated. **D**

6 Fold in the tabs of the interlocking joint at the bottom of the body. Cross the tabs. **E**

7 Fold the feet out to the sides. **F**

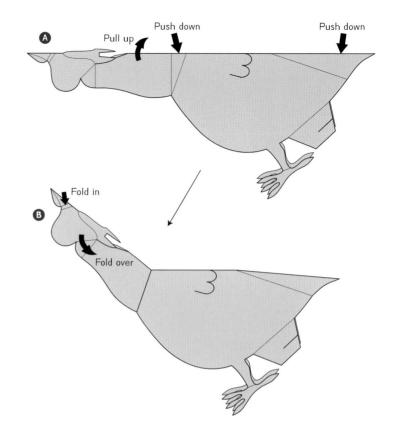

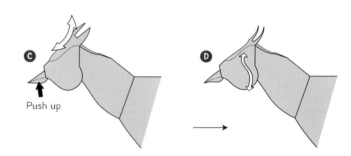

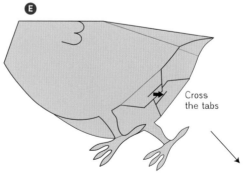

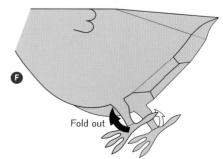

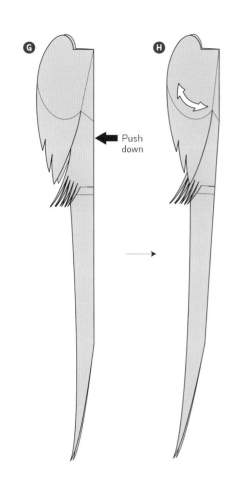

Push
down

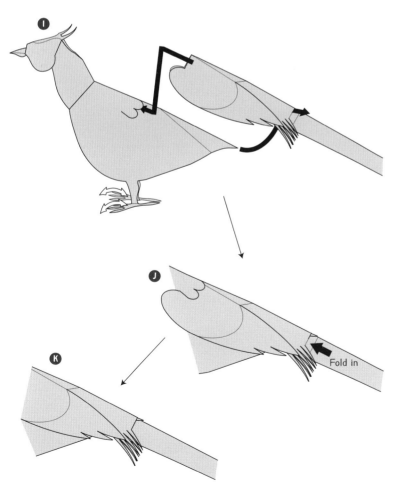

Fold in

8 Fold the wings in half. Push down the back of the wings. **G**

9 Shape the wings following the scored folding lines. **H**

10 Attach the wings to the body by sliding the front end of the wings under the cut on the back and running the tail end of the body through the cut in the base of the tail. Roll the feet over a dowel. **I**

11 Fold in the base of the tail. **J K**

12 Add color to your Pheasant by referencing the project photos. You may want to color the head of the Pheasant with metallic green paint as seen in the photos.

Puffin

The Puffin is a small seabird with a brightly colored beak. The Puffin's unique beak has a hinge-like mechanism that allows the bird to hold a dozen or so small fish at a time.

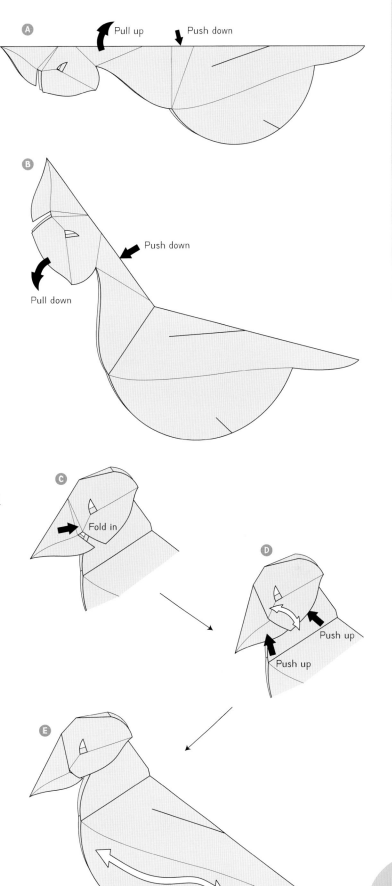

1 Using the Puffin templates on page 117, score the folding lines, then cut along all the solid lines, including the eyes, the cut for the wing joint on the back, the internal cuts of the wings, and the tabs for interlocking joints, as depicted in How to Use This Book on pages 5-13.

2 Fold the template in half using the scored centerline as a guide. Pull up the neck. Pocket fold the bottom of the neck into the shoulders. Ⓐ

3 Pull down the head while you push down and valley fold the top of the head. Ⓑ

4 Fold the base of the beak under the head. Ⓒ

5 Push the cheeks up and out. Roll them over a dowel. Push up the bottom half of the beak. Ⓓ

6 Shape the stomach of the bird following the scored folding lines running across the body. Ⓔ

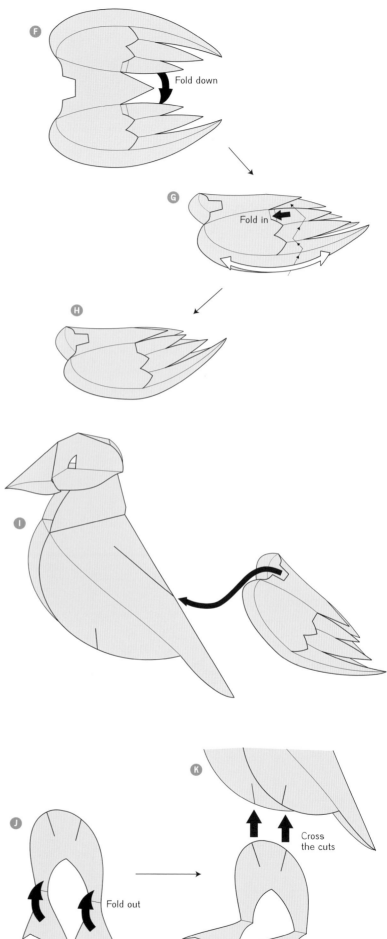

7 Fold the wings in half. **F**

8 Shape the wings following the up-and-down patterns of the feathers. Fold in the smallest feather at the top. **G H**

9 Attach the wings to the body by sliding the front end of the wings under the cut on the back. **I**

10 Fold the feet out to the front. **J**

11 Attach the legs to the body by crossing the cuts at the top of the legs and the ones at the bottom of the body. **K**

12 Add color to your Puffin by referencing the project photos.

Turkey

Turkeys are native to North America, but when the bird was first introduced to Europe in the 1500s, it was shipped from Turkish traders (who brought the bird from America) and referred to as the Turkey Coq.

1 Using the Turkey template on page 118, score the folding lines, then cut along all the solid lines, including the tabs for interlocking joints, as depicted in How to Use This Book on pages 5-13.

2 Fold the template in half using the scored centerline as a guide. Fold the upper body over the hips. **Ⓐ**

3 Push down and pocket fold the base of the tail into the hips. **Ⓑ**

4 Pull up the neck and turn it over. **Ⓒ**

5 Open up the head and turn it over. **Ⓓ**

6 Pull down the snood, and push up the base of the beak. **Ⓔ**

7 Fold the wings over the shoulders. **Ⓕ**

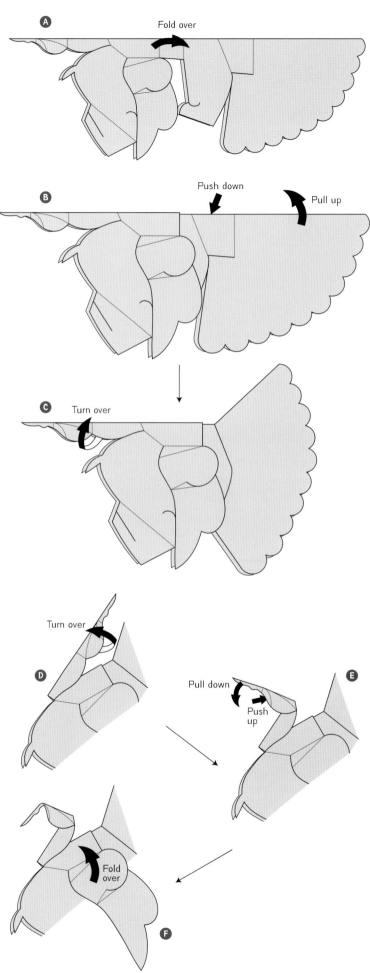

8 Cross the tabs of the interlocking joints to connect the chest and the hips. **G**

9 Fold the wings back down. **H**

10 Push in the lower half of the wings, and fold the upper half of the wings over the shoulders. **I** **J**

11 Cross the tabs of the interlocking joint at the bottom of the body. **K**

12 Roll the chest over a dowel. Apply a small amount of glue to the inside of the feather (the "beard") on the chest. Glue two of them together. **L**

13 Add color to your Turkey by referencing the project photos.

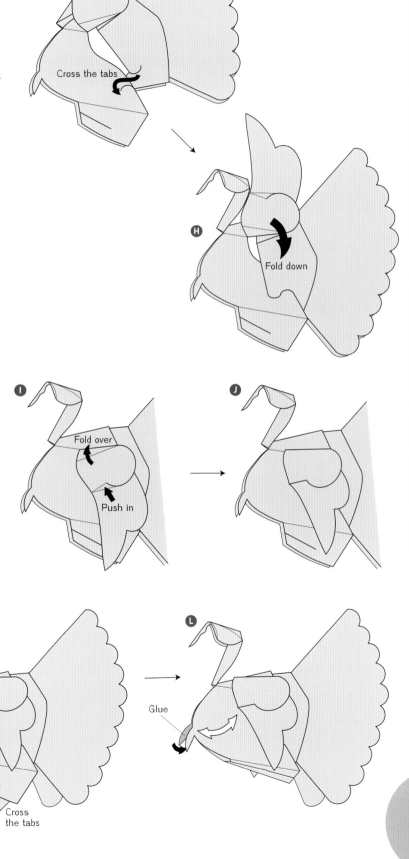

Woodpecker

The Woodpecker has a strong bill for drilling and drumming on trees and a long sticky tongue for extracting insects. This drumming also works to announce territories, create nest cavities, and attract mates.

1 Using the Woodpecker templates on page 119, score the folding lines, then cut along all the solid lines, including the cuts around the eyes, the cut for the wing joint on the back, the feathers on the head, the internal cuts in the wings, and the tabs for an interlocking joint, as depicted in How to Use This Book on pages 5-13.

2 Fold the template in half using the scored centerline as a guide. Fold the bottom of the neck into the shoulders. **A**

3 Pull the head down and over the top of the neck. **B**

4 Fold the base of the beak into the head. Push up the cheeks. **C D**

5 Fold in the tabs of the interlocking joint at the bottom of the body. Cross the tabs. **E**

6 Fold the feet out to the sides. Shape the area between the legs and the tail by following the scored folding lines. **F**

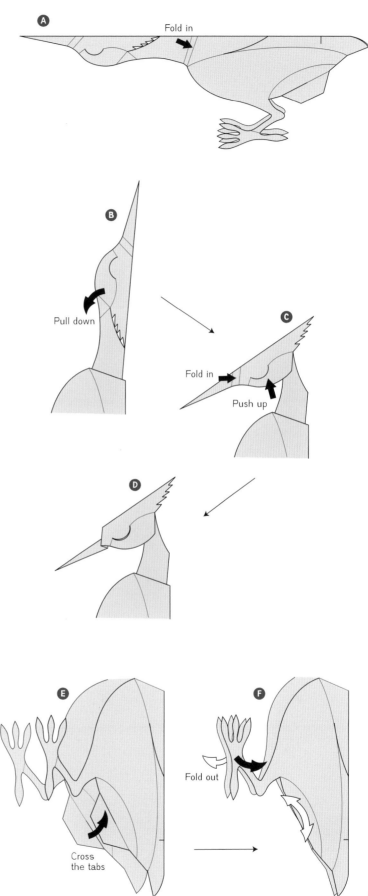

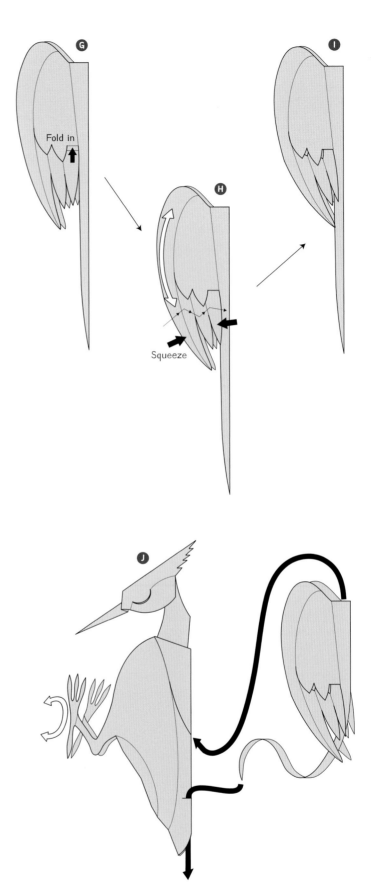

7 Fold the wings in half. Fold in the smallest feather as illustrated. **G**

8 Shape the wings following the up-and-down patterns of the feathers. **H** **I**

9 Attach the wings to the body by sliding the front end of the wings under the cut on the back and running the long tail through the cut at the end of the body. Roll the feet over a dowel. **J**

10 Add color to your Woodpecker by referencing the project photos.

11 To display your Woodpecker, you will need a vertical base. One possible design is depicted in the photos and discussed in Display Methods on pages 12 and 13.

Bald Eagle

Bald Eagles are not actually bald but have white feathers on their heads. In Native American cultures, the birds are considered spiritual messengers from the gods and a symbol of fertility and peace.

1 Using the Bald Eagle templates on pages 120 and 121, score the folding lines, then cut along all the solid lines, including the line around the eyes, the zigzag lines around the neck, the cuts for the wing connection on the back, and the tabs for the interlocking joints, as depicted in How to Use This Book on pages 5-13.

2 Fold the body in half following the scored centerline. Fold the neck over the shoulders. Push down the tail feathers. **Ⓐ**

3 Push in the base of the beak under the eyes. Push back the beak and fold it over the sides of the face. **Ⓑ**

4 Fold down the tip of the beak. Push up the lower half of the beak. Roll the back of the head over a dowel to round it. **Ⓒ Ⓓ**

5 Pull up the tabs of the interlocking wing joints and cross the tabs with the bases of the wings. **Ⓔ**

6 Fold the wings in half from the scored centerline. **Ⓕ**

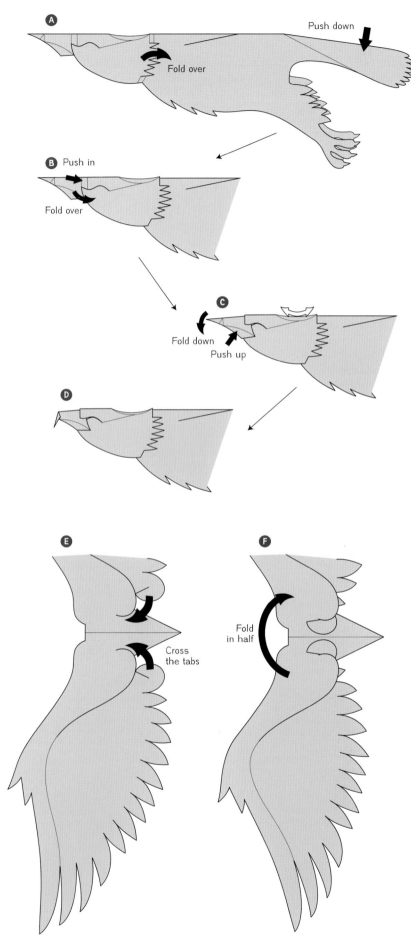

82

7 Push aside the triangle piece on the back of the eagle's body. Insert the pointed end of the wings into its opening. Make sure the bases of the wings are completely placed in this opening. **G**

8 Place the triangle piece of the eagle's back into its original position over the bases of the wings. **H**

9 Shape the wings following the scored folding lines on them. Roll the talons of the eagle over a dowel to shape them. **I**

10 Color your Bald Eagle, using the project photos for reference.

11 If you want to display your Bald Eagle flying, run the thread through the X marked on the wings.

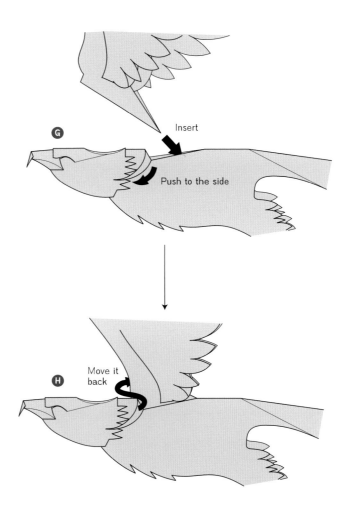

Macaw

Macaws are colorful birds native to Mexico, Central America, and South America. They are said to have the intelligence level of an eight-year-old and the emotional level of a two-year-old.

1 Using the Macaw templates on pages 122 and 123, score the folding lines, then cut along all the solid lines, including the cuts for the wing joints, the internal lines of the wings, and the tabs for an interlocking joint, as depicted in How to Use This Book on pages 5-13.

2 Fold the body in half using the scored centerline as a guide. Pull down the head while you push down and valley fold the back of the neck. Push down the tail. **A**

3 Roll the sides of the head over a dowel to add more curves to them. Bring the tabs for the interlocking joint to the middle, and then cross the tabs. **B**

4 Fold down the beak, first at the base and then the tip. They are both pocket folds. **C D**

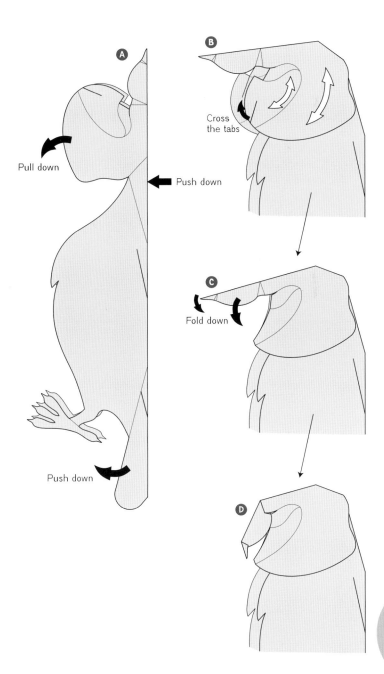

Pull down

Push down

Push down

Cross the tabs

Fold down

Tip

Macaws are very colorful birds. To make your Macaw, start with card-stock in a dominant color for the particular bird you want to make and add patches of other colors later on.

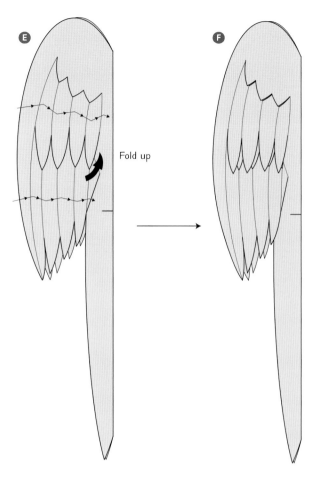

Fold up

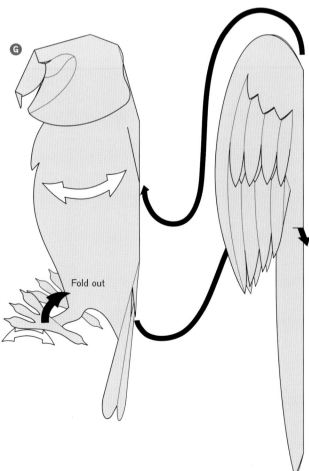

Fold out

5 Fold the wings in half and shape them following the up-and-down patterns of the feathers. Fold up the bottom half of the wings toward the back. **E** **F**

6 Round the body over a dowel. Attach the wings to the body by sliding the front end of the wings under the cut on the back and running the tail end of the body through the cut in the long tail. Fold the feet out and roll them over a dowel. **G**

7 Adjust the angle of the legs so that your Macaw will stand comfortably. The long tail of the Macaw is meant to hang lower than the feet. Display the bird on a base or on a tree branch.

8 Add color to your Macaw by referencing the project photos.

Peacock

The tail feathers of the Peacock are pigmented brown, but the feathers' structural coloration makes them appear iridescent blue, turquoise, and green, depending on the light angle.

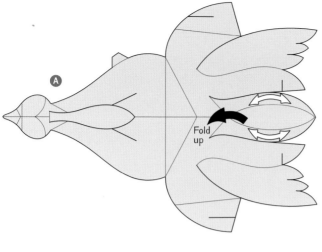

A

Fold up

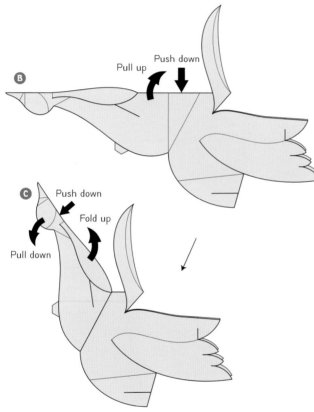

B

Pull up   Push down

C   Push down

Fold up

Pull down

1 Using the Peacock templates on pages 124 and 125, score the folding lines, then cut along all the solid lines including the crown on the head, the patterns inside the spread tail feathers, and the tabs for interlocking joints, as depicted in How to Use This Book on pages 5-13.

2 Fold up the tail and shape it following the scored folding lines. Fold the body in half using the centerline as a guide. **A**

3 Pull up the neck while you pocket fold the bottom of the neck into the shoulders. **B**

4 Pull down the head while you push down and valley fold its top. Fold up the crown. **C**

5 Roll the crown around a dowel to coil it. Fold the base of the beak into the head. **D**

6 Cross the tabs of the tail joint. **E**

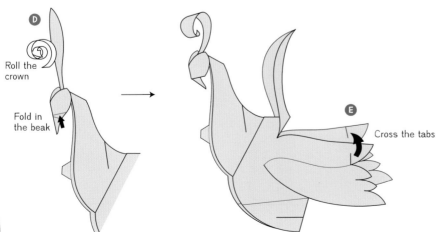

D

Roll the crown

Fold in the beak

E   Cross the tabs

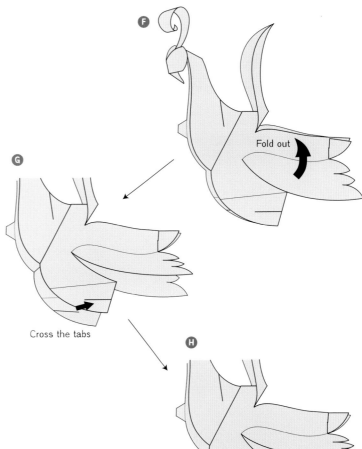

7 Fold out the wings to the sides. **F**

8 Fold in the tabs of the interlocking joint at the bottom of the body. Cross the tabs. **G** **H**

9 Fold the back feathers over the spread tail. **I**

Cross the tabs

Fold over

10 Cross the cuts at the bottom of the back feathers and the ones on the back of the neck. **J**

11 Apply a small amount of glue to the outside of the tab on the neck. Fold it in and glue it to the inside of the other half of the neck. Shape the spread tail feathers following a "folding fan" type of pattern. **K**

12 Add color to your Peacock by referencing the project photos. The Peacock in this book was made with metallic vellum paper and colored with metallic paint.

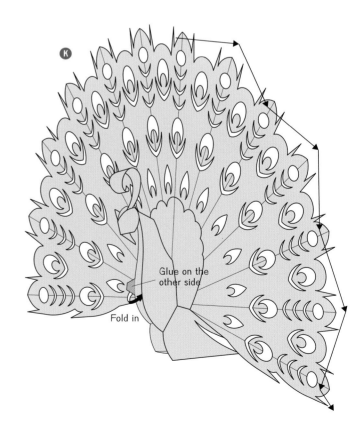

Glue on the other side

Fold in

Shoebill

The Shoebill is known for its large, shoe-shaped bill and its slow movements, but it moves with remarkable speed once it spots its favorite meal, the African lungfish.

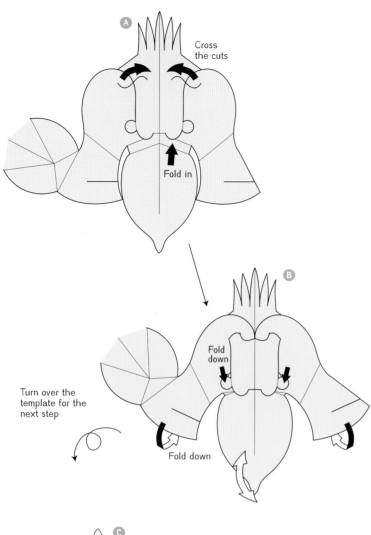

Cross
the cuts

Ⓐ

Fold in

Fold
down

Ⓑ

Turn over the
template for the
next step

Fold down

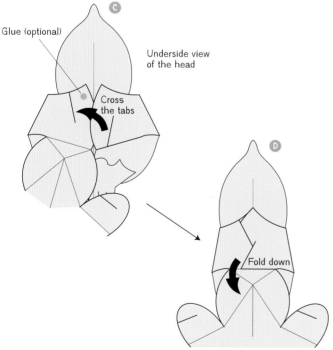

Glue (optional)

Cross
the tabs

Underside view
of the head

Ⓒ

Ⓓ

Fold down

Note: For this project, the printed folding lines will be visible on the head surface of the completed bird but not on the rest of the body.

1 Using the Shoebill templates on page 126, score the folding lines, then cut along all the solid lines, including the lines around the eyes, the internal cuts of the wings, and the tabs for the interlocking joints, as depicted in How to Use This Book on pages 5-13.

2 Fold the base of the bill into the head. Cross the cuts on the sides of the head and the ones at the top of the head. Ⓐ

3 Fold down the eyes. Fold down the underside of the head. Roll the tip of the bill over a dowel to round it. Turn over the template for the next step. Ⓑ

4 Cross the tabs of the interlocking joint under the head. For a more secure connection, you may apply a small amount of glue in the spot indicated in the illustration. Ⓒ

5 Fold down the entire head toward the chest. Ⓓ

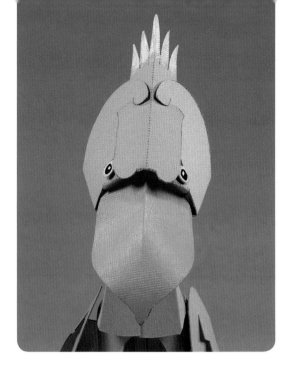

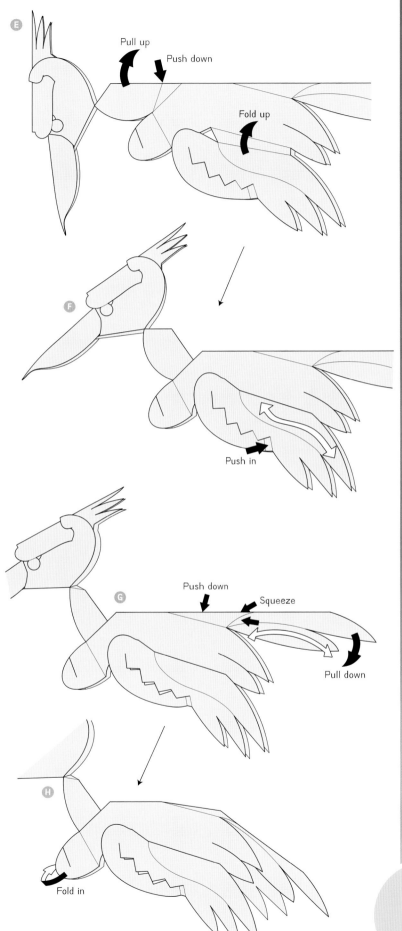

6 Fold the body in half using the scored centerline as a guide. Pull up the neck while you pocket fold its bottom into the shoulders. Fold up the wings toward the back. **E**

7 Shape the wings following the folding lines in the middle. Push in the end of the cut in the wings as described in the illustration. **F**

8 Squeeze in the base of the tail. Shape the tail following the folding lines. Push down the entire tail from the hips. **G**

9 Fold in the tabs for the chest joint. **H**

93

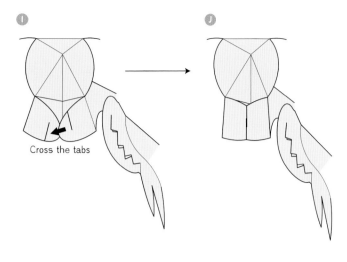

Cross the tabs

10 Cross the tabs. ❶ ❶

11 Squeeze the legs in half. ❶

12 Fold in the hips using the scored center-line as a guide. Fold the feet out to the front. ❶

13 Connect the legs and the body by wedging the bottom of the body through the cuts at the top of the hips. Adjust the angle of the legs to achieve a good balance so the bird can stand on the ground (both feet and the tips of the wings should be touching the ground). For a more secure connection, apply a small amount of glue in the spots indicated in the illustration. Roll the feet over a dowel. ❶

14 Add color to your Shoebill by referencing the project photos.

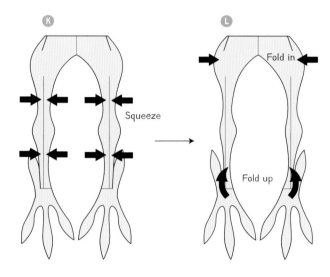

Squeeze

Fold in

Fold up

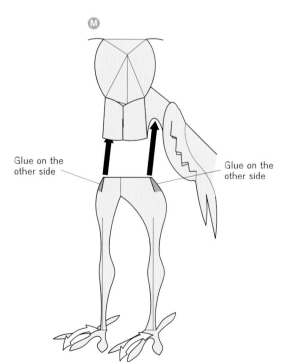

Glue on the other side

Glue on the other side

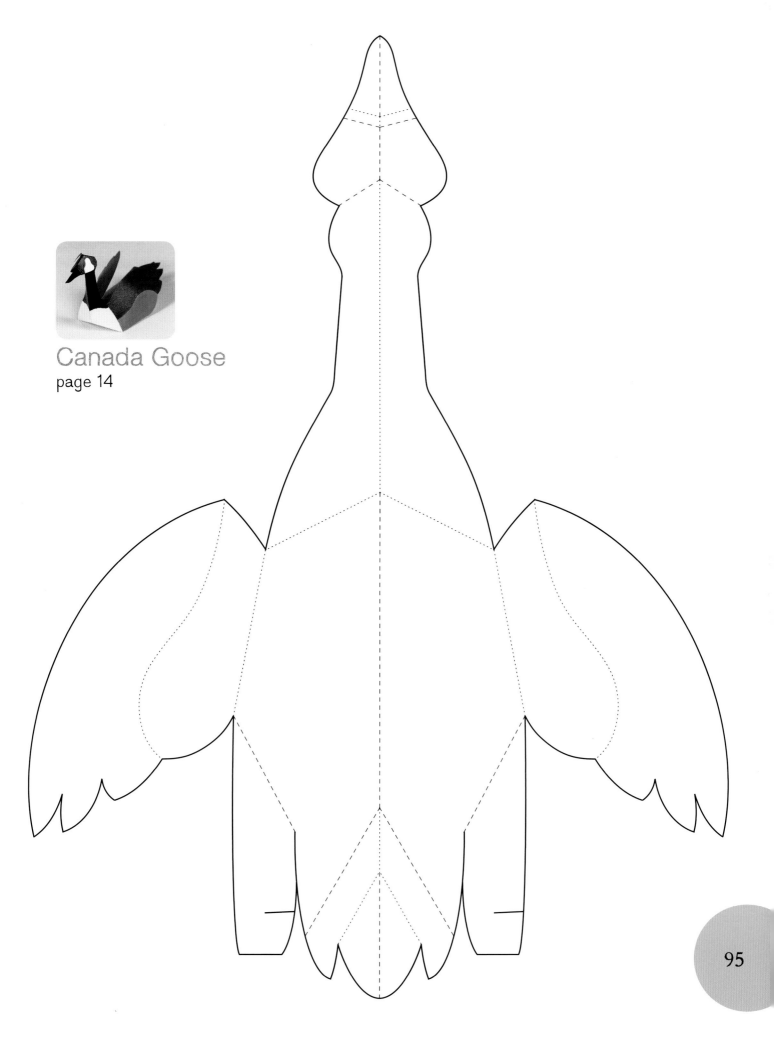

Canada Goose
page 14

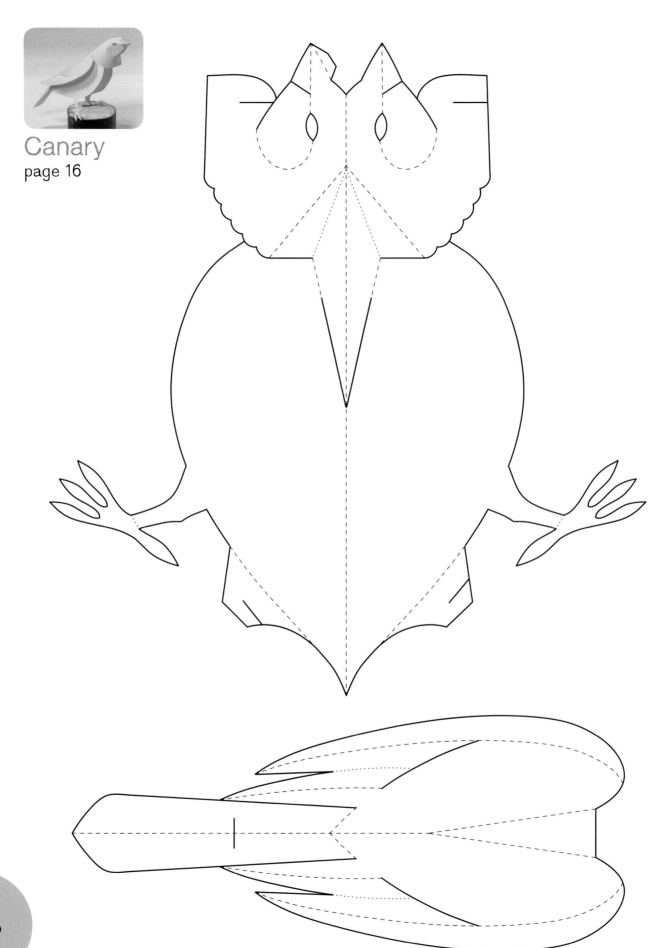

Canary
page 16

Crow
page 19

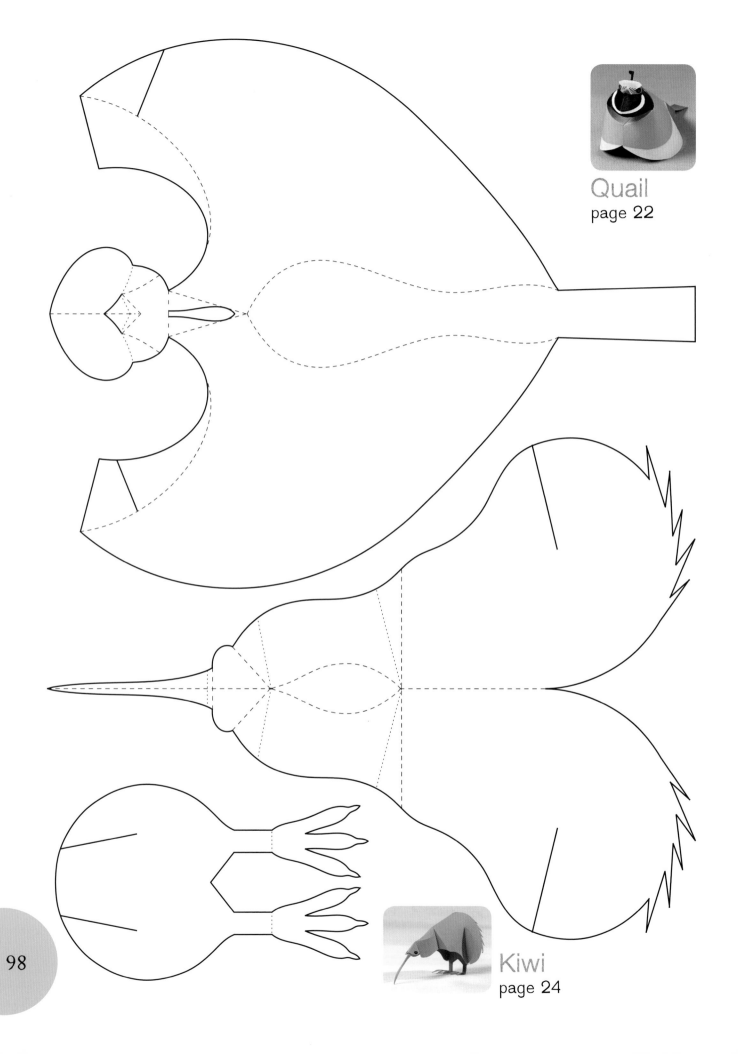

Kiwi
page 24

98

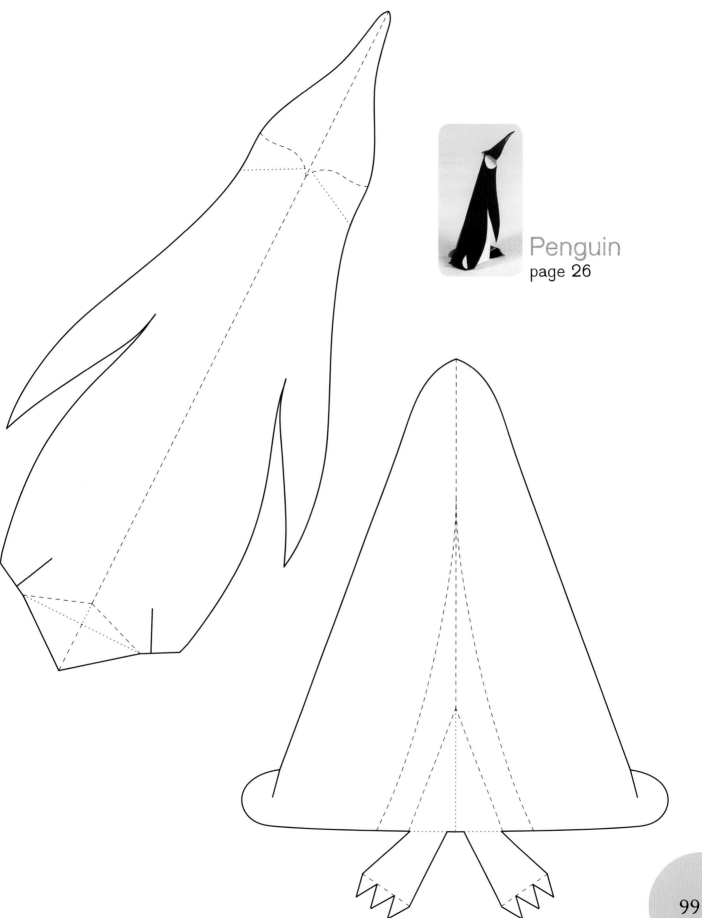

Penguin
page 26

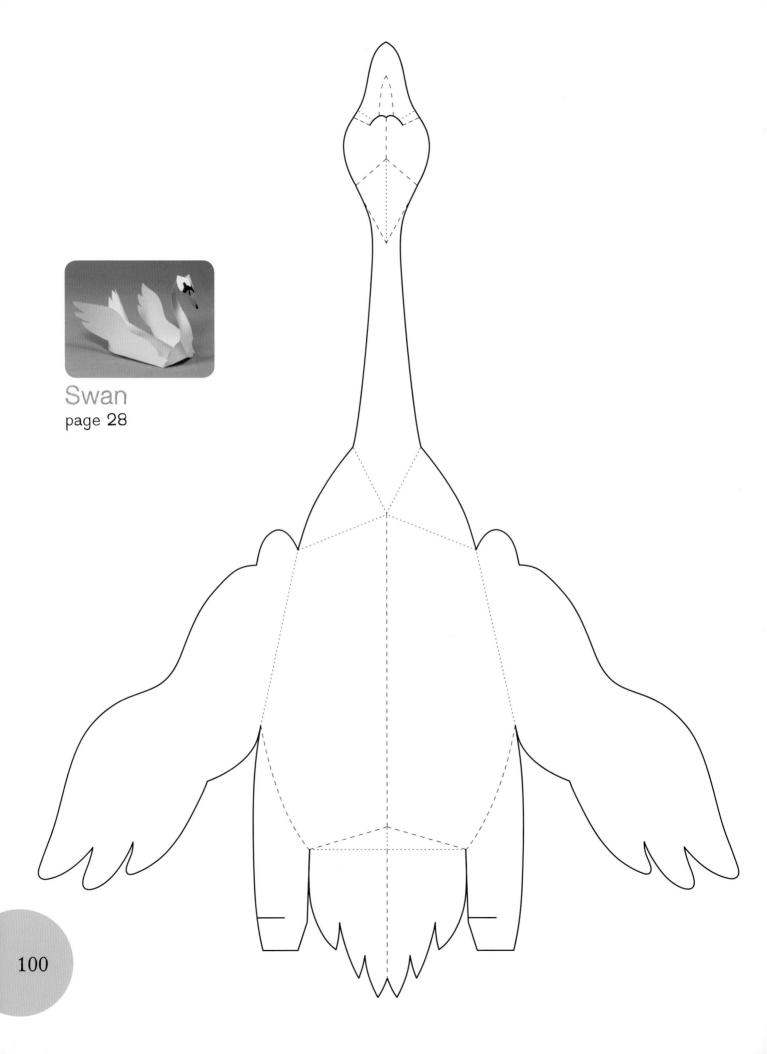

Swan
page 28

100

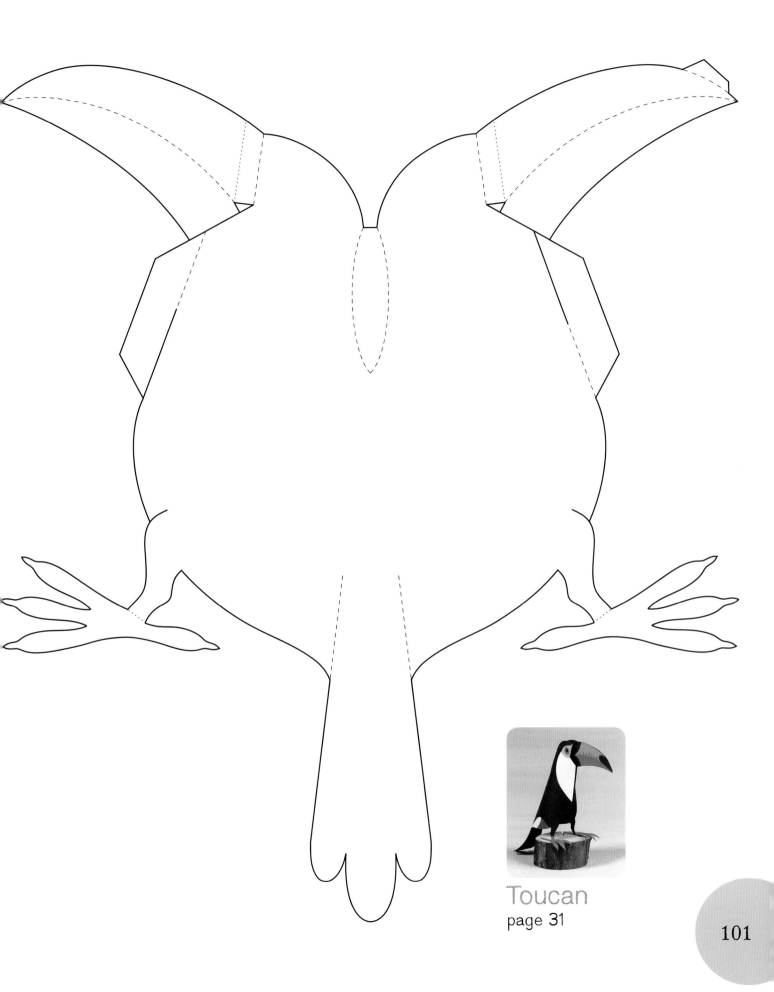

Toucan
page 31

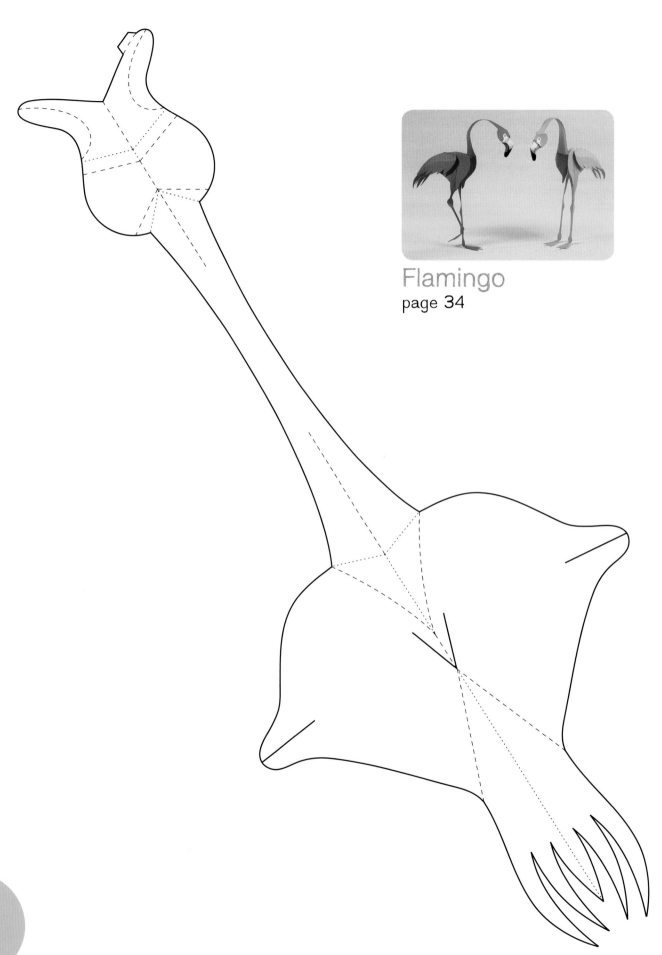

Flamingo
page 34

102

Straight legs version

One leg bent version

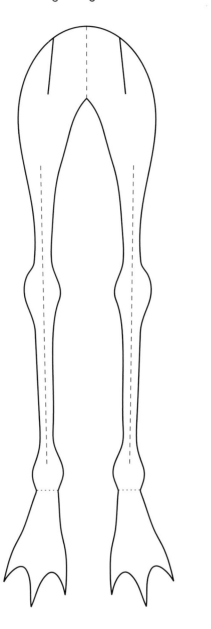

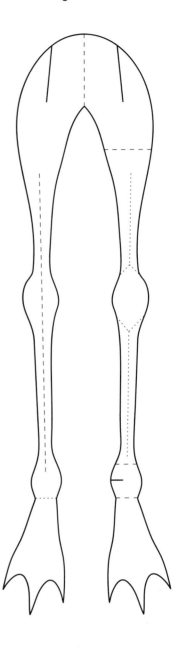

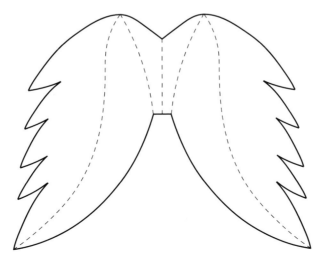

103

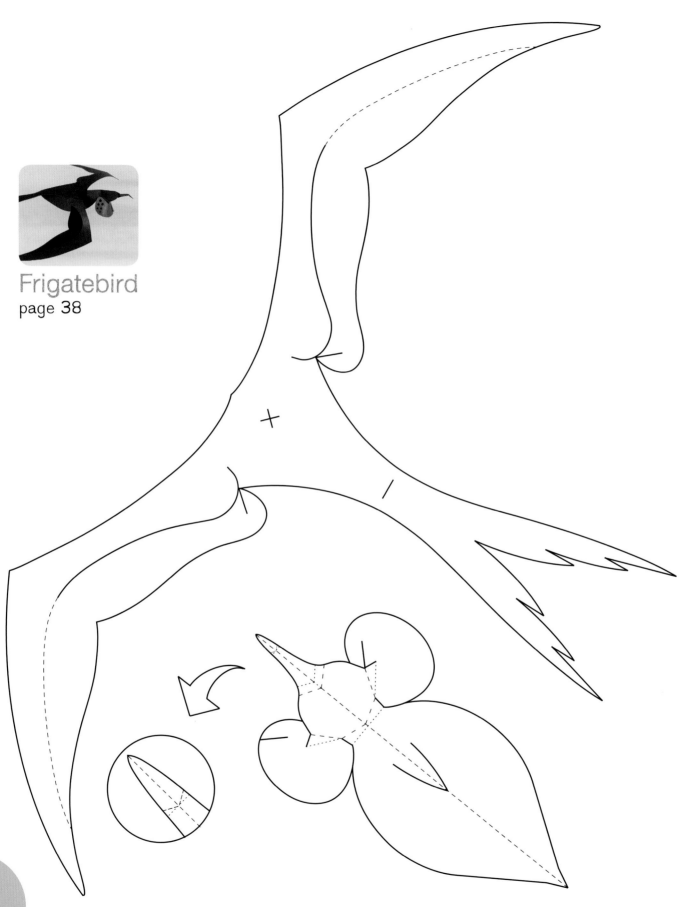

Frigatebird
page 38

104

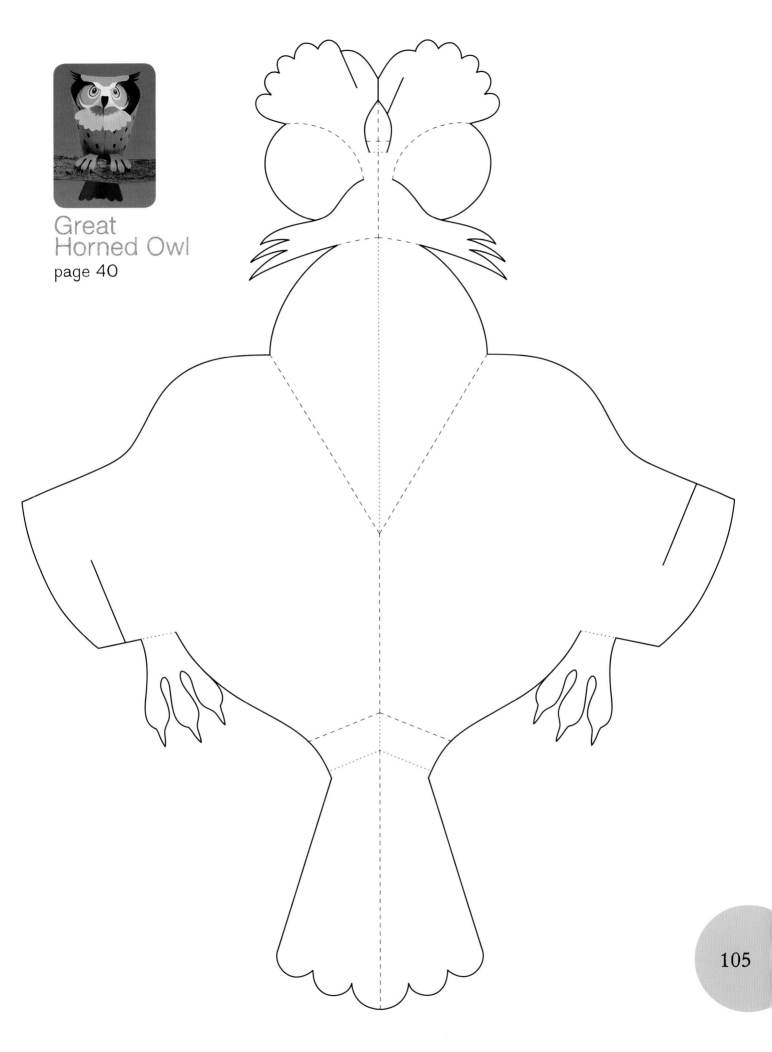

Great
Horned Owl
page 40

105

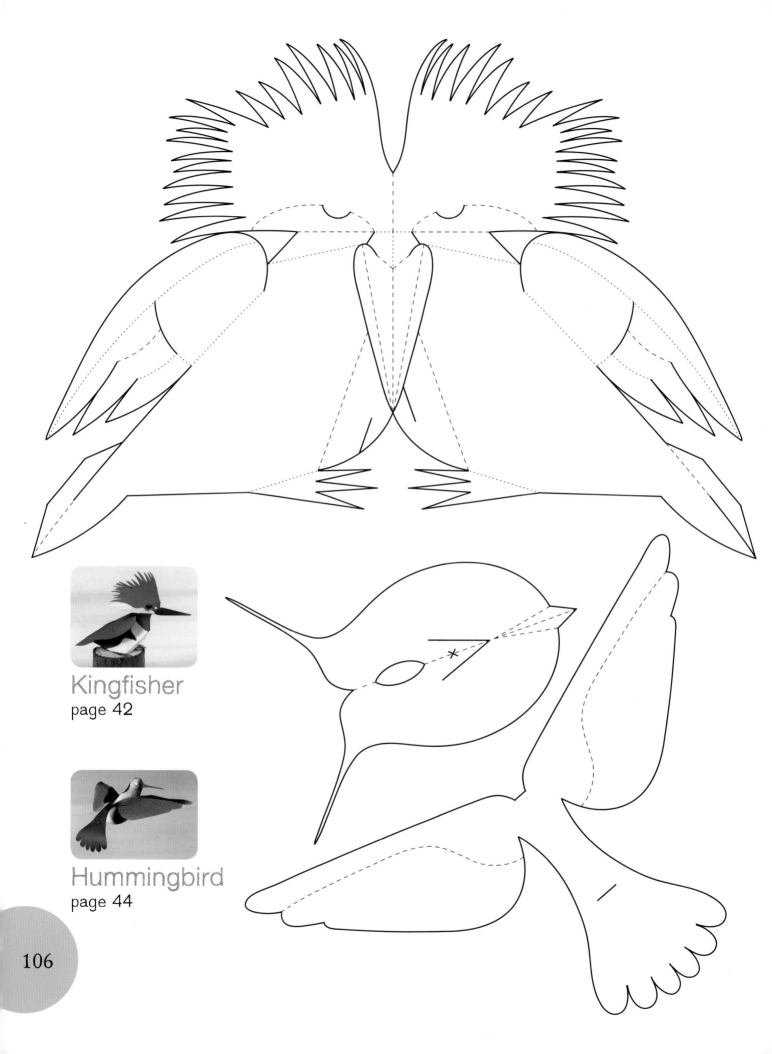

Kingfisher
page 42

Hummingbird
page 44

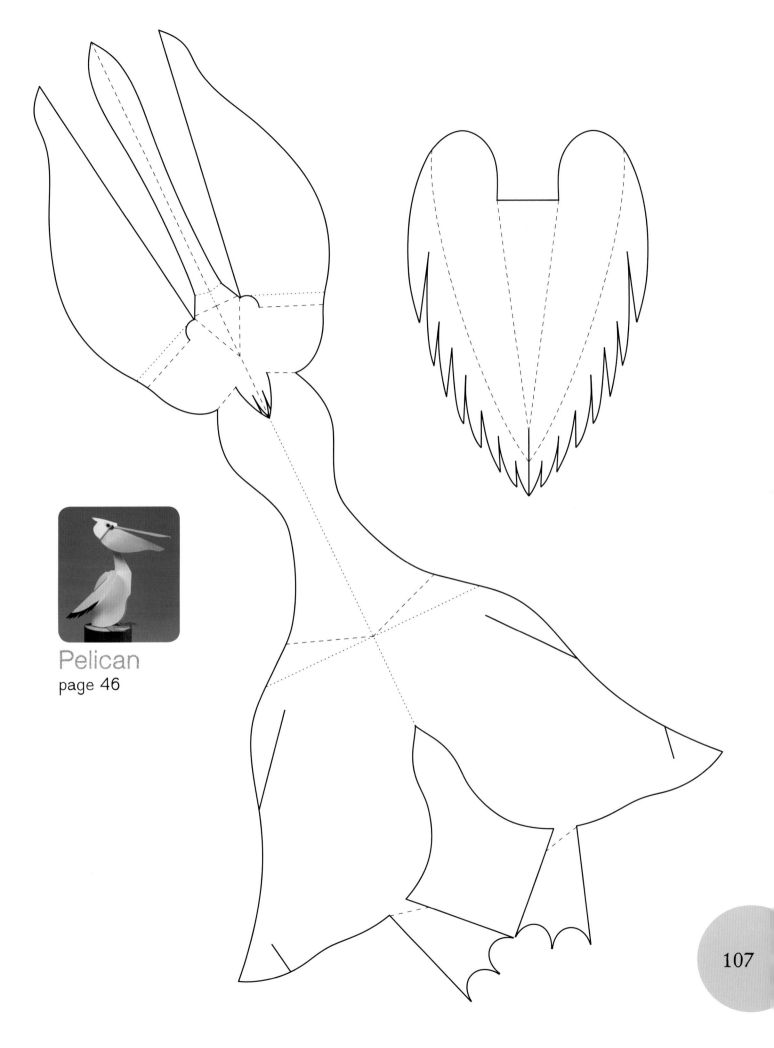

Pelican
page 46

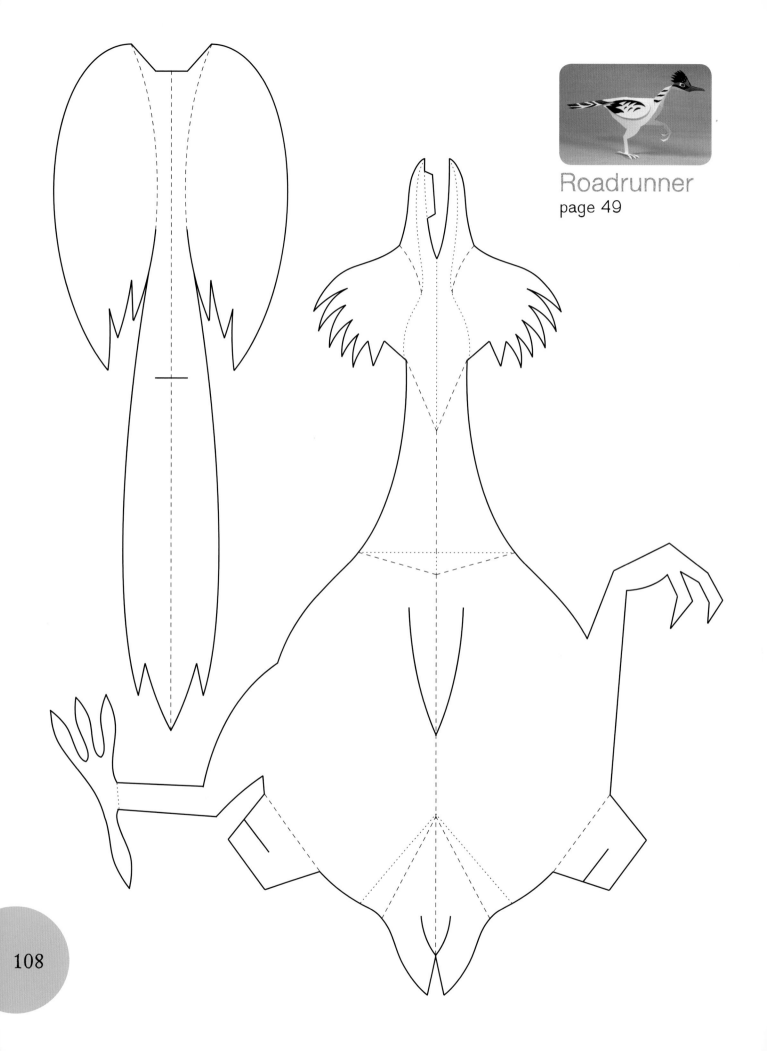

Roadrunner
page 49

108

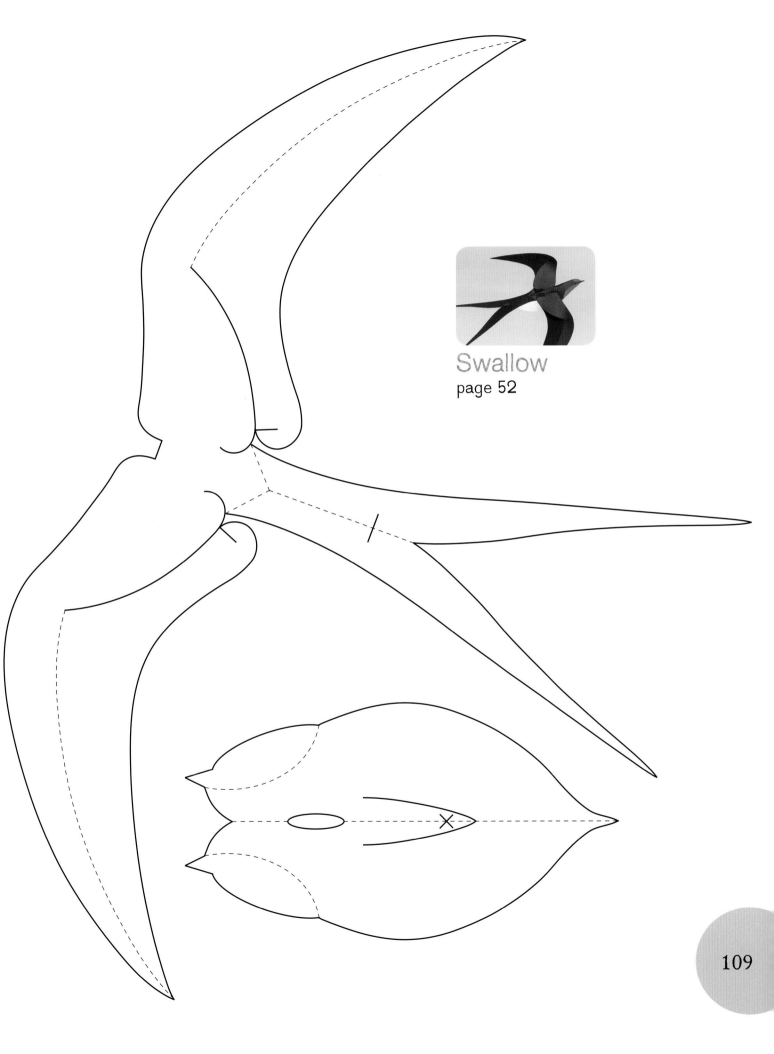

Swallow
page 52

109

Dove
page 54

Dodo
page 56

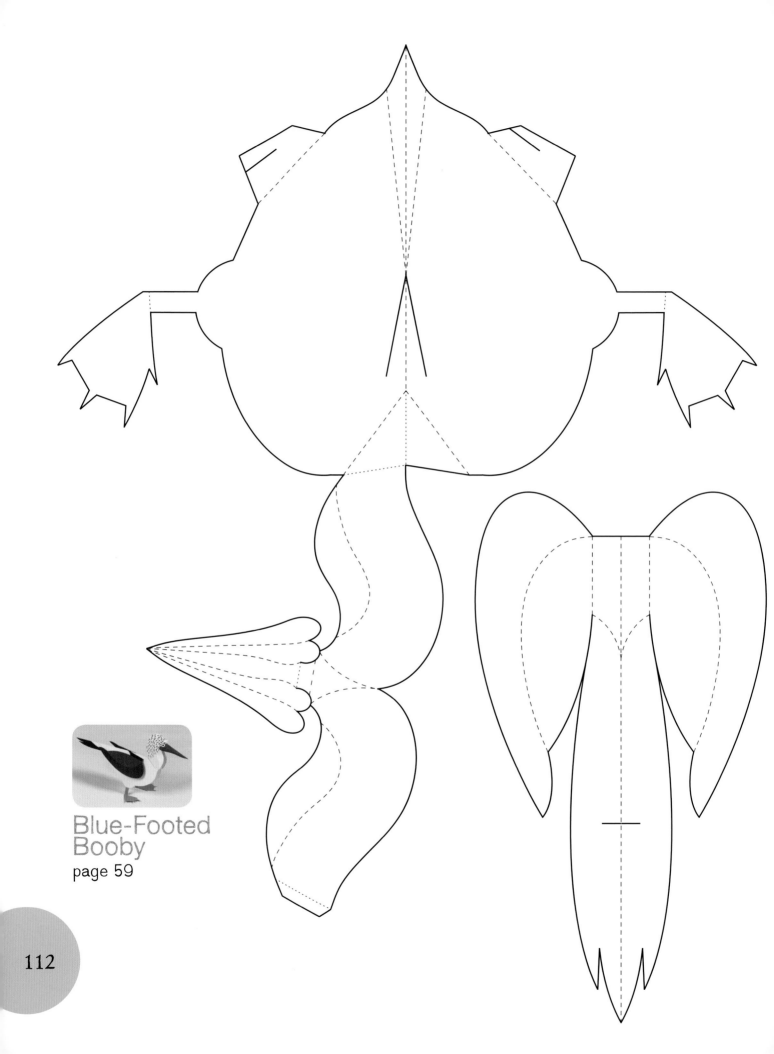

Blue-Footed
Booby
page 59

112

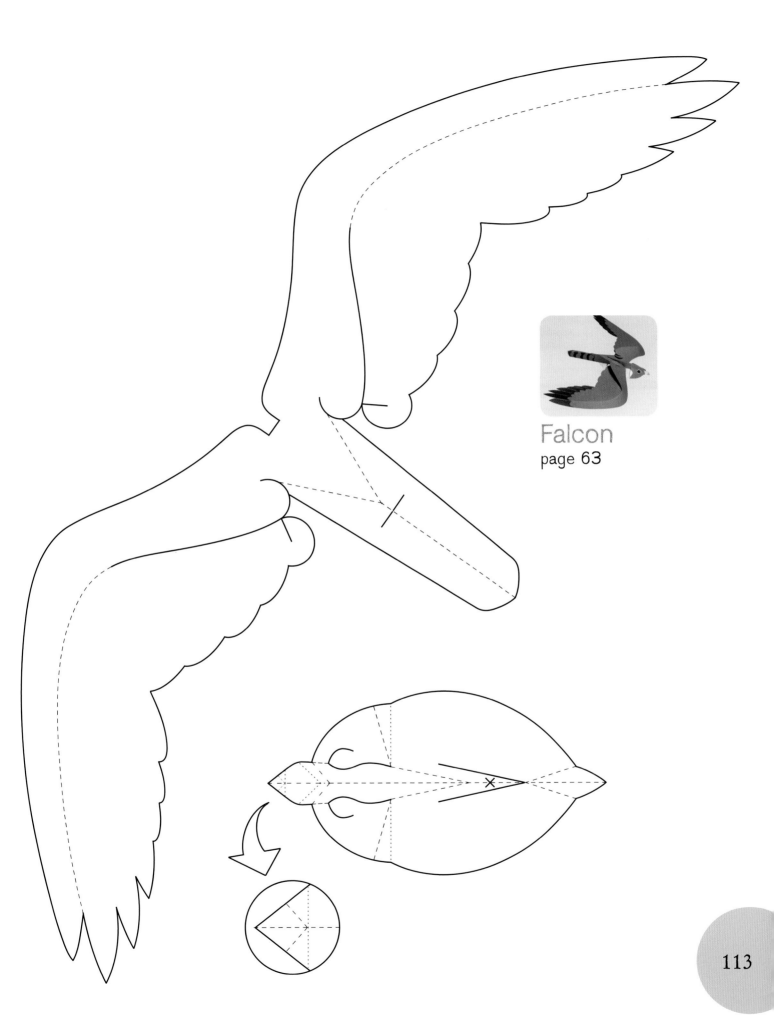

Falcon
page 63

113

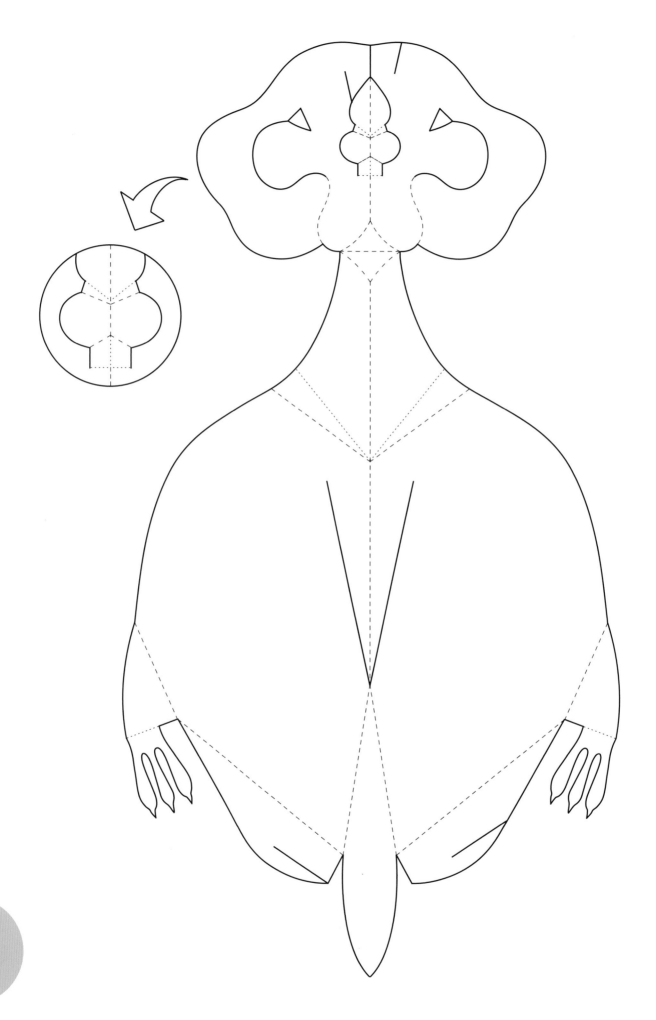

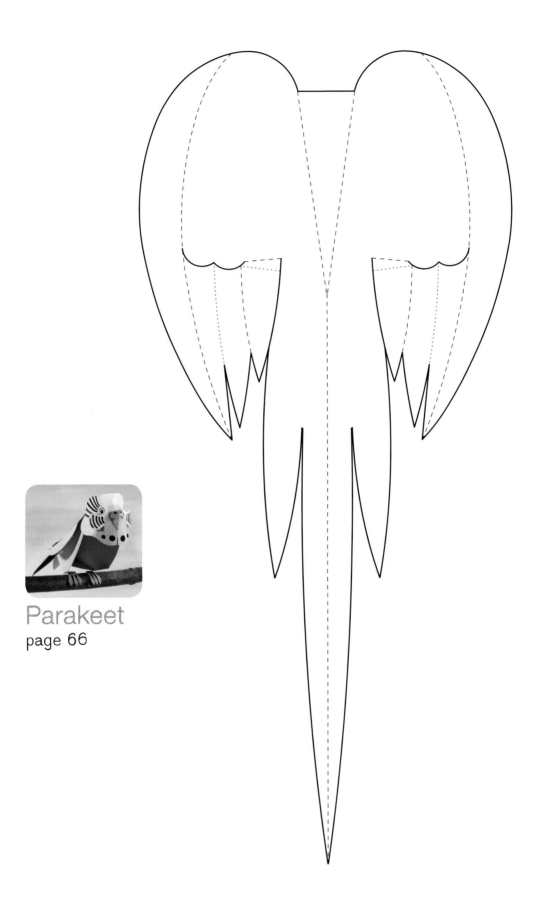

Parakeet
page 66

115

Pheasant
page 69

116

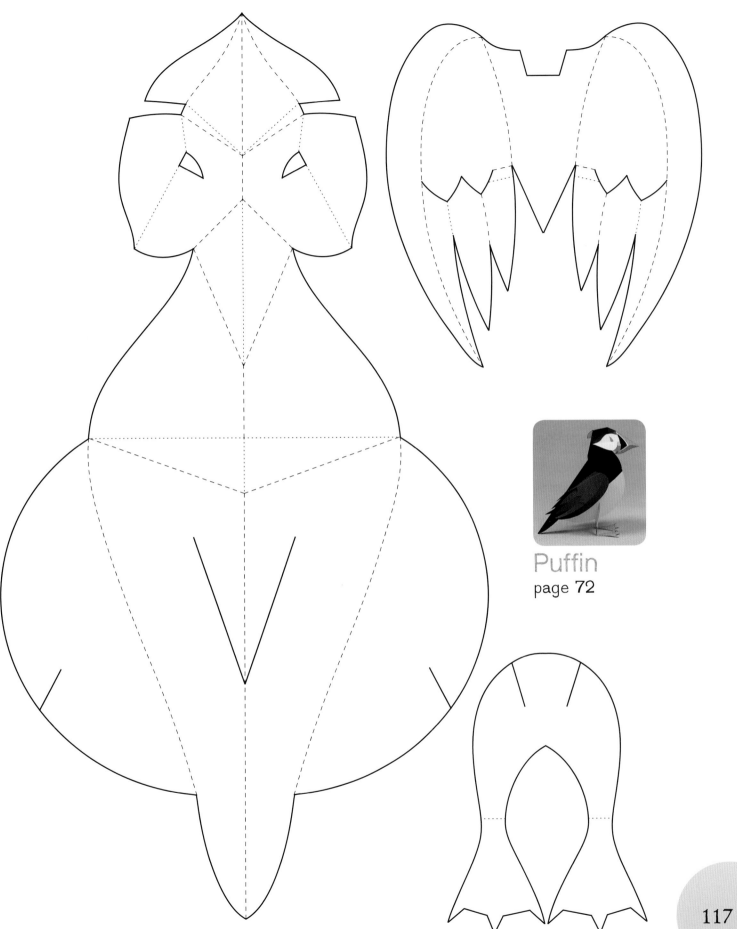

Puffin
page 72

117

Turkey
page 75

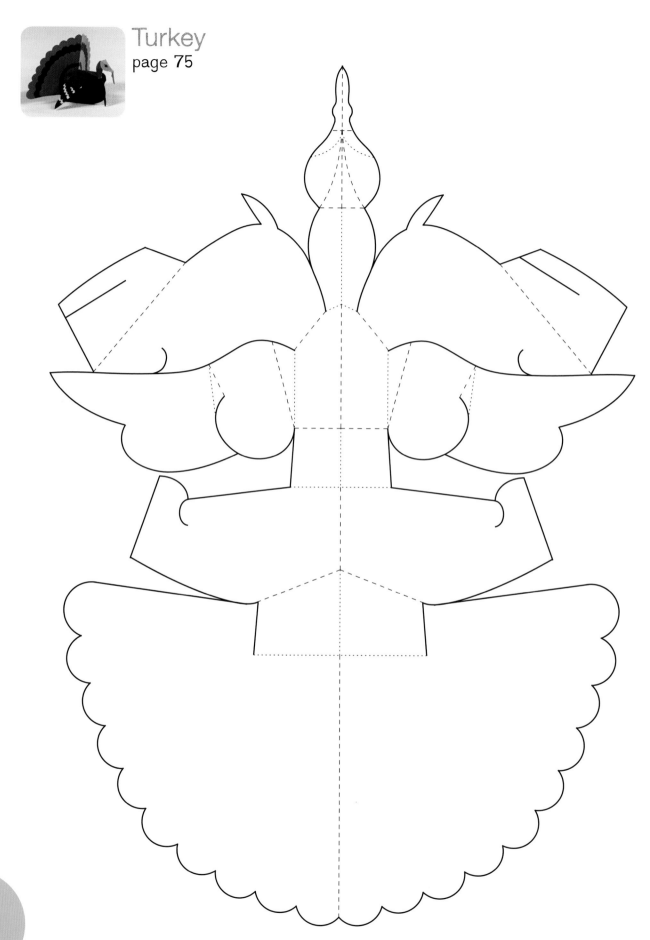

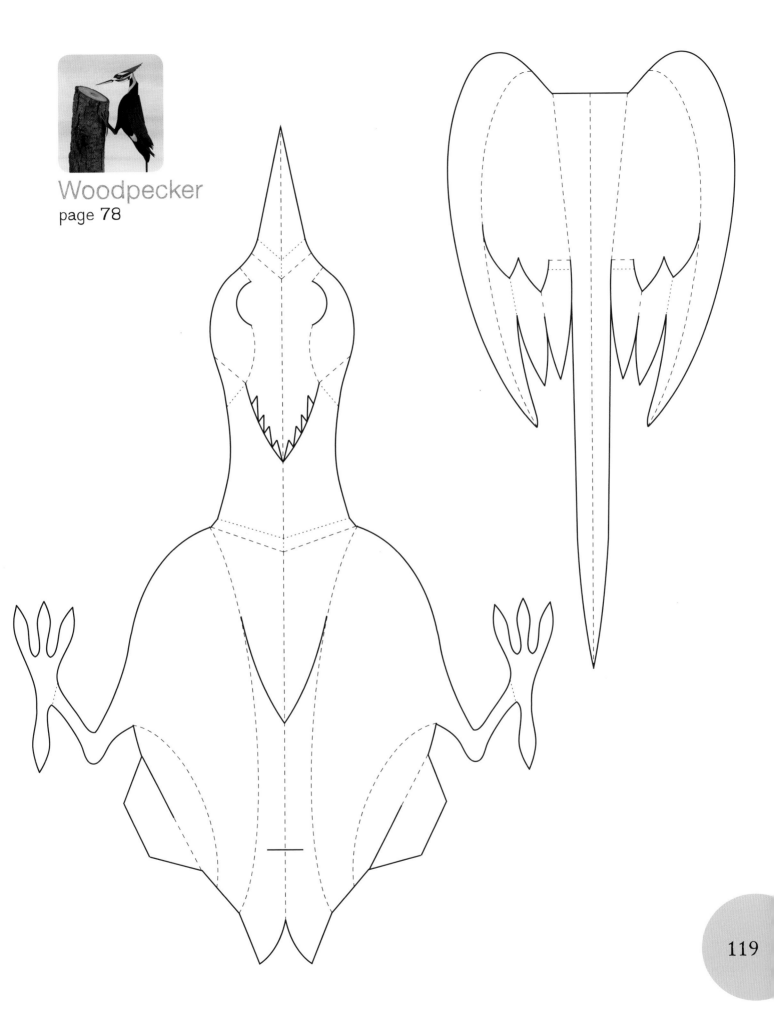

Woodpecker
page 78

119

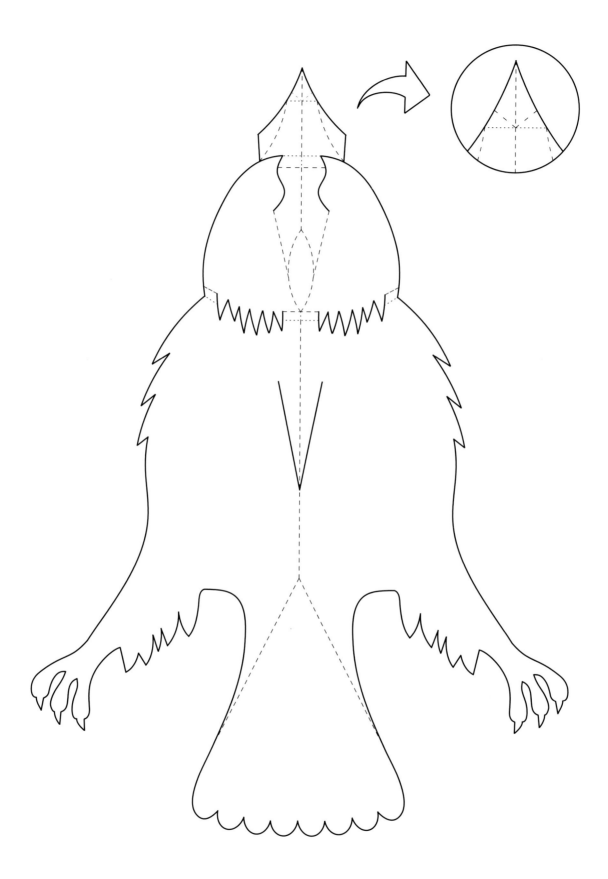

Bald Eagle
page 81

121

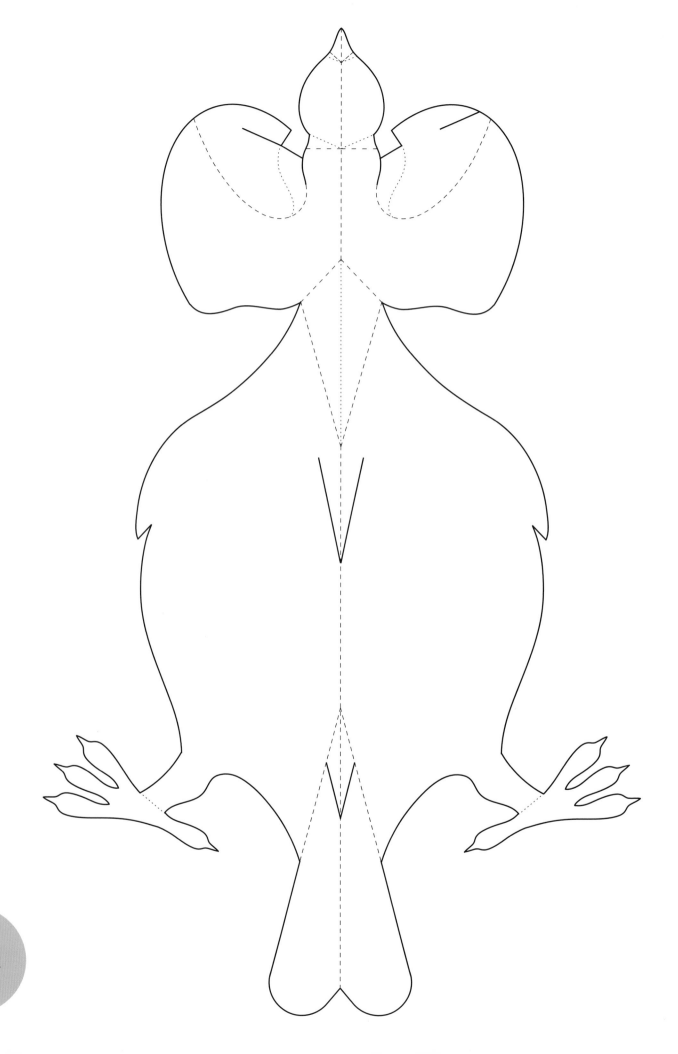

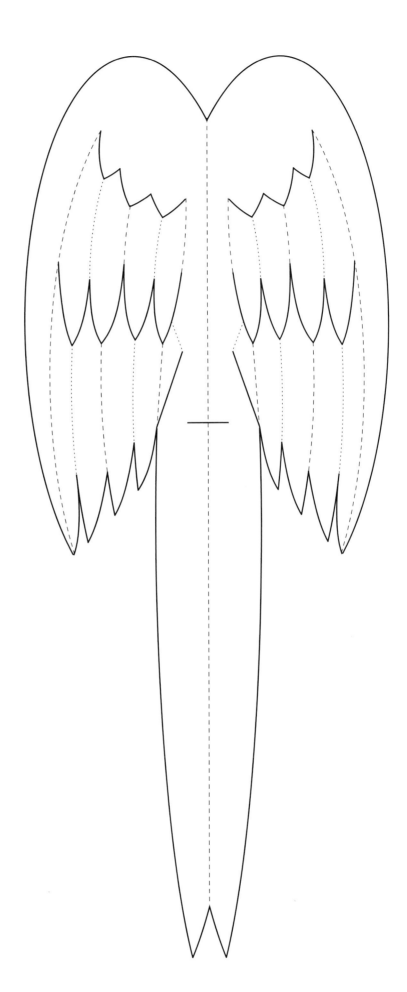

Macaw
page 84

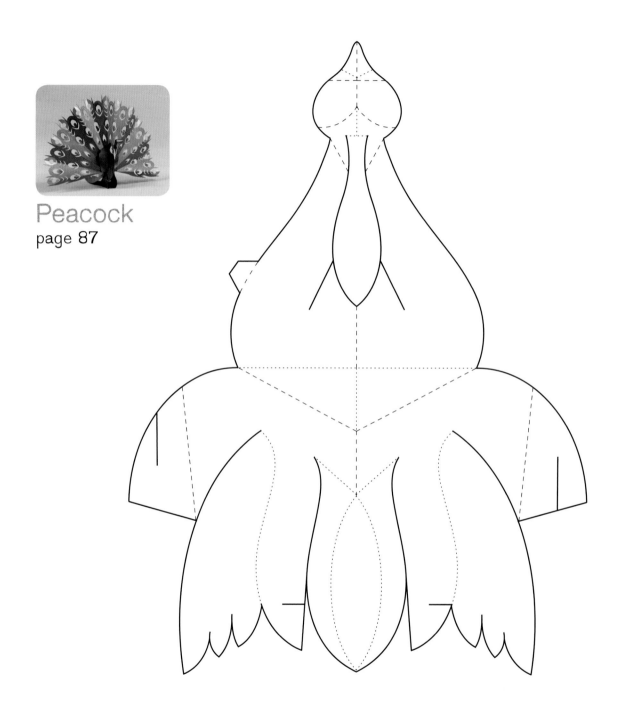

Peacock
page 87

124

Shoebill
page 91

ABOUT THE AUTHOR

Hiroshi Hayakawa was born and raised in Japan. After receiving a BA in French Literature at Keio University in Tokyo, he moved to the United States in 1991 to attend the Columbus College of Art and Design in Columbus, Ohio. After earning BFAs in Photography and Fine Arts, he received his MFA in Photography at Cranbrook Academy of Art in Michigan. Hiroshi began making kirigami animal sculptures in the mid-90s when he was asked to create table decorations for a Chinese New Year party. He teaches drawing and basic, intermediate, and mixed media photography at the Columbus College of Art and Design. Hiroshi's photography is represented by the Sherrie Gallerie in Columbus, Ohio. He is the author of *Kirigami Menagerie* (Lark, 2009) and *Paper Pups* (Lark, Spring 2013). Hiroshi lives in Columbus, Ohio, where he works professionally with photography and sculpture.

ACKNOWLEDGMENTS

I would like to express my sincere gratitude to the following people; without your help, this book wouldn't have been possible.

Thank you to all of the people at Lark Books and Sterling Publishing who were involved in the production of this book. Special thanks goes to:

Nicole McConville for giving me a chance to work on this wonderful project. Writing this book was truly a joy.

Linda Kopp for your excellent advice and strong support. Your encouragement gave me a little peace of mind when things were difficult.

Shannon Yokeley for your work in the photo session and your book design. Your energy, positive attitude were infectious. I truly admire your persistence for perfection.

Kristi Pfeffer for your design direction. You gave me wonderful insights into photographic compositions from an editorial standpoint. They made so much sense to me.

Kathy Sheldon for your great work as a copy editor. Your eagle eye and logical thinking made this book read much more smoothly.

Steve Mann for your great photography and your patience when Shannon and I requested countless lighting adjustments during the photo session.

My wife, Nanette, for being patient with me when I hardly came out of the studio for a few months while working on this book.

Ms. Chilin Yu for your inspiration and encouragement. You instilled the idea of this book in my head many years ago.

INDEX

BONUS ONLINE PROJECTS

Find more paper birds projects
online at www.larkcrafts.com/bonus.

Hen

Duck

Condor

Waldrapp

Albatross

Barn Owl

Cockatiel

Crowned Crane

Rooster

BOOK CREDITS

Editor: Linda Kopp
Art Director: Shannon Yokeley
Illustrator: Hiroshi Hayakawa
Photographer: Steve Mann
Cover Designer: Shannon Yokeley